VALOUR AND VALUES

Aligning Military Experiences to CSR

TESTIMONIAL

"Brig. Rajiv Williams' *"Valour and Values: Military Experiences in CSR"* is an insightful exploration of the intricate connections between Army Social Responsibility (ASR) and Corporate Social Responsibility (CSR). With a clear focus on aligning ASR initiatives with the Sustainable Development Goals (SDGs) and the ESG framework, this book serves as a crucial resource for both military leaders and corporate practitioners. This book is a valuable guide for those committed to fostering such change."

—Mr. Narayana Murthy, Founder – Infosys Limited

I have read the book– "Valour and Values – aligning military experiences to CSR" authored by Brig Rajiv Williams, YSM in awe and with great admiration. It has very succinctly meshed military values and experiences in the social good of communities thereby impacting lives of people in a positive way. I found the reading very contemporary with meaningful expressions boldly analyzed and a way forward for corporations to support military projects through their CSR funds by not just doling out money with a possible intent of gaining favour. An exhaustive read in one go.

—Lt. Gen. Satish Dua, PVSM, UYSM, AVSM, SM –
Former Chief of Integrated Defence Staff (CISC)

"In this book, Former Brigadier, Mr. Rajiv Williams, has managed to masterfully juxtapose and align the intricate paradigm of Army Social Responsibility (ASR) with the broader concept of Corporate Social Responsibility (CSR). Mr. Williams has also seamlessly incorporated his lived experiences to explore the intersection of military ethos with societal well-being nuancedly. This book will be a seminal contribution to the field of both CSR and ASR and is a must-read for professionals as well as students who wish to become the path bearers to achieving transformational success through the concept of value-driven and thoughtful leadership. This book will enable us to relook, rethink and recalibrate our understanding towards compliance, sustainable development, and the discourse of CSR and our knowledge of ASR."

—Professor (Dr.) C Raj Kumar Founding Vice Chancellor,
O.P. Jindal Global University

In *"Valour and Values – Aligning Military Experiences to CSR"*, Brig. Rajiv Williams draws on his extensive experience as a former Army officer and Group Head of CSR at Jindal Stainless, India's largest stainless steel company, to offer a unique perspective on Corporate Social Responsibility. By connecting military values with corporate initiatives, Rajiv demonstrates how the discipline, leadership, and social commitment of the armed forces can power impactful CSR projects. This insightful book also emphasizes the importance of documenting and reporting CSR efforts, ensuring accountability, and mapping out the road ahead for businesses committed to social good.

—Parul Soni, Global Managing Partner, Think Through Consulting (TTC), and Founder & Secretary General, Association of Business Women in Commerce & Industry (ABWCI)

An amazing book titled "Valour and Values – aligning military experiences to CSR", authored by Brig Rajiv Williams, YSM (Retd). I have known Brig Williams for long and greatly appreciate the way he has documented various CSR practices based on his military experience. Very candid in his thoughts and relevant in his approach in developing CSR projects in sync with Company philosophy of Sustainable CSR. This is a distinct shift from earlier corporate practices by carrying out activities around welfare and philanthropy. Interesting and helpful references. A must read.

—Mr. Ashwini Saxena, CEO, JSW Foundation

The book 'Valor and Values', thoughtfully penned by my father, a die-hard Fauji, highlights the close interplay between the core values integral to the Indian Army and how they can be utilized for the upliftment of society in general, and the underprivileged in particular. The narrative discusses the success of various CSR projects involving health, agriculture initiatives, and social entrepreneurship, which would not have been possible without key Indian Army values such as discipline, integrity, selflessness, and inclusivity. It is a must-read for anyone embarking on a journey in the social sector, offering insights into the complexities at play and strategies to achieve the best results in an ever challenging and dynamic environment.

—Dr Kanishka Williams, MBBS, MS, FRACS, FAOrthA, Consultant Orthopaedic Surgeon and Head of Department, Alice Springs Hospital, Central Australia Health Service Northern Territory Government

VALOUR AND VALUES

Aligning Military Experiences to CSR

Brig. Rajiv Williams, YSM (Retd.)

Foreword by

Dr. Bhaskar Chatterjee

Former Secretary GoI, Ministry of Corporate Affairs

Former Director General Indian Institute of Corporate Affairs

CEO Anil Agarwal Foundation, Vedanta

PENTAGON PRESS LLP

First published in 2025 by
PENTAGON PRESS LLP
206, Peacock Lane, Shahpur Jat
New Delhi-110049, India
Contact: 011-26490600

Typeset in AGaramond, 12.5 Point
Printed by Aegean Offset Printers, Greater Noida

ISBN 978-81-980002-8-6

www.pentagonpress.in

DEDICATION

This book is dedicated to the Indian Army, which made me understand the various attributes required in the making of an 'officer and gentleman'. It is important for an officer to understand the overall architecture of conflict management with conflict prevention being the preferred option rather than conflict resolution, while carrying out assigned roles and responsibilities. It is important to understand the relevance of looking after the interests of local communities by sharing military resources. A first step in Army Social Responsibility (ASR).

I dedicate the book to Mrs. Deepika Jindal of the Jindal Stainless Group, who gave me space and the opportunity to initiate Corporate Social Responsibility activities in the largest stainless steel company in India. In doing so, I could strengthen my belief in the corporate-community connect, which in some ways had similar outcomes as experienced in the Army – the concept of Corporate Social Responsibility (CSR).

Most importantly, I dedicate the book to my wife Vineeta and our son, Dr. Kanishka, who encouraged me to put my thoughts to paper. Despite the challenges that a wife of an infantry officer has to go through, Vineeta stood by me and had a great part in ensuring it was completed.

CONTENTS

Appendices: Highlights/Extracts of Important Government of India Notification

FOREWORD

I feel a great sense of pleasure and happiness to be asked to write the foreword for this path-breaking work on the novel concept of Army Social Responsibility. These feelings stem from the fact that I have known Brig Rajiv Williams for more than two decades now, not only as a much-decorated officer of the Indian Army but as a masterful implementer of CSR projects and a true champion of Human Rights. On his retirement from the Army, he devoted himself to social causes and found his true calling in the newly developing field of "strategic Indian CSR".

We were involved together in the drafting of the CSR legislation and rules that were incorporated under Section 135 of the Companies Act of 2013. Many of his perspectives on what CSR as a concept can do for the development agenda of our nation, helped me to formulate my own ideas on what the entire *strategic approach* should be and how the "new look CSR" should be different and distinct from the earlier approach of philanthropy and "generally doing good." His clear vision of a people-centric approach where the individual disadvantaged and marginalised person becomes the epi-centre of corporate "give-back", gave shape and substance to the formulation of the overall policy that emerged from the deliberations of the Drafting Committee.

Brig Williams, as Head of the CSR operations of a large Corporate House, distinguished himself as a true practitioner of the letter and spirit of the legally mandated Indian CSR. Some of the projects that he initiated and oversaw the implementation of, deserve to go down in the annals of best practices. His flair for innovation, timely implementation and outcome-orientation, deserve the highest commendation. He fully drew upon his experience in the Indian Army and the orientation he derived therefrom, to the practice and performance of CSR.

In this book, Brig Williams has painstakingly and imaginatively crafted the concept of Army Social Responsibility. How does the Army, in its peace time existence, help serve the common citizen? How does it put itself to the service of the needy and the marginalized among our society in the same way that it puts itself to the service of the nation in times of war? How does an army man relate to civilian needs? In times when natural calamities strike, how does the Army step in and render yeoman service in relief and rescue operations? In other words, how does the Army with its vast resources of highly competent manpower, machinery and equipment and technical capabilities, prove immensely useful when the civilian establishment is severely challenged? These and many related questions are answered by Brig Williams in this exceptional book with great clarity and lucidity.

There is another aspect of CSR that relates to the Army; and this has been growing by leaps and bounds over the last decade. The Army through its enlightened leadership, has been able to attract fairly large sources of corporate funding to the conduct of CSR projects by NGOs. In these areas, where the Army is engaged in interactions with the community, CSR has proved to be a great means by which divisive forces have been contained and turned into uniting and cohesive initiatives. This is particularly evident in Jammu and Kasmir, Ladakh and in key areas of the Noth East. These projects have enabled the Army to reach out to the community and demonstrate how together, peace and harmony can be ushered in and maintained even in areas where there is terrorist activity, strife or ethnic tensions. The three-way relationship between the Army, corporate entities and civil society organizations is indeed a unique experiment that has unleashed the hidden potential of community bonding, mutual understanding and peaceful intent.

What Brig Williams has done, through the modus of writing this book, is to flesh out a thought process that is both unique and seminal. It has never been articulated before, nor ever crystallized so clearly. It adds both a new dimension as well as a new paradigm to the ever-widening circle of CSR research and knowledge. The perspectives he has brought to the subject, are, of course unique, but I remain positive that this work, will spur others to debate, discuss and above all, recognise Army Social Responsibility as a field of study and learning.

Dr. Bhaskar Chatterjee
Former Secretary GoI, Ministry of Corporate Affairs
Former Director General Indian Institute of Corporate Affairs
Former CEO Anil Agarwal Foundation, Vedanta

PREFACE

As a young Army officer, I often wondered why military men in uniform were engaged in carrying out activities that were responsibilities of civilian government officials co-located in the same areas. Why should army troops, besides carrying out their prime responsibilities of patrolling, manning posts and other military duties, also be given additional responsibilities to provide facilities to civilians located close to military stations and posts? While some activities like levelling areas for making playgrounds for local communities and schools were understandable, yet when there were requirements like deputing educational personnel from military units to help local schools, organize health camps in remote areas, when civilian government health staff were available, etc., were difficult for me to comprehend – the 'why' of such add-on tasks. Stark fault lines between the military and civilian government officials posted in the same area or close by were visible and the hostile reactions of civilians who were being supported by the military were quite challenging for me to understand, especially when I was posted in the remote parts of Kashmir and the Northeast.

Immediately after the 1971 Indo-Pak war, after we captured large tracts of area near Shakargarh in the Western Theatre; I, then a Second Lieutenant, was given the responsibility of escorting Pakistani civilians – most of them old, infirm and children, across the ceasefire line to Pakistan. They had been abandoned by the

Pakistani military guarding the area and by their own families just minutes before we captured their villages. It was hard for me to question the action of pushing these civilians across the line and realized that they had been totally neglected by Pakistani soldiers, who merely took advantage of them in various ways as informed by the very people I escorted. There was a distinct break in relationship between these people and their military mentors deployed in the area. On withdrawal, without caring as to who was being left behind, Pakistani soldiers took along with them the fit and sturdy men and women for their personal gain.

Many years later, when I became a middle level and senior officer, I reflected upon the initial years in uniform and of my first civilian encounter during war and realized that the military is deployed in difficult areas to guard the borders and to protect the lives and property of people in the vicinity of our deployment. Despite the fact that many negative overtures were made by the very people we were helping, yet it was important, as part of the 'conflict prevention strategy' for the military to respect the communities around the area of deployment and share military resources with them. There were operational advantages in such acts as there were times when the civilians provided timely information to troops during infiltration attempts made in the 'area of responsibility'.

To illustrate the point, I narrate an incident soon after the Kargil war of mid-1999, when I was commanding an infantry brigade at Drass. There were a number of initiatives started for civilians as part of the Army's 'Sadbhavana' project, an exercise in 'winning hearts and minds', in the Drass-Kargil region. The respect we earned from the locals was noteworthy with genuine gratitude from the locals. Soon after the Pakistani-sponsored terror attack on the Indian Parliament on 13 December 2001, 'Op Parakram' was launched by the Indian Army and tensions rose high between India and Pakistan, with regular shelling from Pakistan on our troops. We were preparing for the 'Kargil Vijay Diwas (Day)' celebrations at Drass and a number of high senior military and civilian personnel were expected to come to the site to pay their respects to the martyrs killed during the Kargil war in the area below the famous Tololing feature there.

As a part of the innovative security measures taken by the Army, instructions were conveyed to deploy a few soldiers wearing local outfits at the heights to keep a watch on probable infiltrators from across the line of control. Since we had a good relationship with the locals, all the villages were informed to be on the lookout and inform the nearest military post. As part of my local tour of the area, I had barely left my brigade headquarters towards Drass when I was stopped by some locals who informed me that villagers had reported having seen unfamiliar faces, with weapons, on the mountain tops. Surprised by such an action by locals, I told them that they were possibly misinformed as no such information had been received by our intelligence agencies. My headquarters were contacted about the inputs received from the locals and was promptly informed that the men the villagers had seen on the mountain tops were our own disguised as civilians. I appreciated their concern and realized how important it was for the military to be connected with civilians in the area of deployment – *The importance of 'Army Social Responsibility.*"

Not long thereafter, I took premature retirement from the Army and joined the development sector and was inducted into the Jindal Stainless Group as the Group Head, Corporate Social Responsibility (CSR). This was just being initiated in corporates with activities aimed at the locals. The chasm seen between the industry and the people who were displaced from their houses was evident and required the corporates to do some social good to create employment opportunities for them. This was a shift from the earlier stand on doing charitable and philanthropic activities to getting connected with the local community through various projects and programs and in the process to remove social discord and mistrust. *The start of a new norm – 'Corporate Social Responsibility'.*

It is in this context that I pen my thoughts from the initial learning of Army social responsibility as I transitioned into the civilian world and furthered the concept of corporate social responsibility. I believe that unless there is a symbiotic relationship between the two entities, that is, Army and civil or between the corporates and local communities, the fault lines of progress will become further blurred, which will have a direct impact on the overall growth story of the country.

REFLECTIONS

Lt Gen (Dr) Ranbir Singh
PVSM, AVSM**, YSM, SM (Retd.)
Administrative Member
Tele : 0172-2997895

Armed Forces Tribunal
Regional Bench, Chandigarh
Tank TCP, Chandimandir
Panchkula (Haryana)-134107
Email: ranbirdhatt@gmail.com

Reflections By Lt Gen Ranbir Singh, PVSM, AVSM**, YSM, SM Former Director General of Military Operations and General Officer Commanding in Chief, Northern Command

It is a matter of great honour and privilege for me to write some personal reflections of the amazing work which the Indian Army has been doing toward mitigating the woes and travails of the civilian population impacted by inadequacy of facilities, in the book, which focuses on the relevance of "Army Social Responsibility" (ASR) in the context of "Corporate Social Responsibility" (CSR). The people living or working in areas close to where the Army is deployed look up to the latter for support in times of difficulty, natural calamity or for facilities like education, skill training, health support or perhaps for just exposure visits and so on. It is a kind of a social responsibility, which the Indian Army, wherever possible, undertakes with adequate thought and far sightedness.

It is in this context that military - civic operations like "Operation Sadbhavana", "Operation Good Samaritan" and others under military support to civilians are being carried out in different geographies. The aim of such operations or activities is to provide the locals with requisite support to make their lives comfortable and respectful and I have been a proponent and ardent supporter of the Army undertaking such missions during my stint as the Army Commander of Northern Command, responsible for the entire then the state of Jammu and Kashmir.

My first interaction with the author was in the area of Drass, soon after the Kargil conflict. As the Commanding officer of my Battalion, 9 DOGRA, I understood the need of maintaining good relations with the local people in my area of responsibility. I just felt that sharing select military resources available to me with the civilians in the hour of need, helped people to understand the Army better and not be scared of the soldiers. I remember the time, when the sick and pregnant women were required to be brought to the Primary Health Centre in Drass from the most inaccessible villages and that too during the winter months, when the snow is at its peak and temperatures close to minus 40 degrees Celcius. The choice was to either wait for the local administration to make arrangements, which was nigh impossible or for me to take a decision to send my snow mobile vehicle to bring them to safer abodes where medical emergency could be attended. I opted to deploy the military resource at my disposal and timely evacuation saved the life of the woman in pain. In addition, by providing the local youth with skill training, other livelihood generation activities support, or encouraging sports and at no extra pressure on my command, I found a complete attitudinal change amongst the local population toward the Army, which I must confess earlier was a major concern.

Similarly, during my command at various levels in the Army, I found that such civic responsibilities made the people realize that they could depend upon the Army in case of a situation beyond their control. As an Army Commander, I got immense satisfaction when my command undertook rescue operations during floods and other disasters whenever those hit the State. It was a bond that did leave a lasting impact on the people affected and supported by the uniform fraternity.

Post my retirement, as a sitting Administrative Member in the Tribunal, I reflect upon what the Indian Armed forces can do to address problems of the civilian community in partnership with the local and Central government machinery and I am convinced that it is not only a good thing but the right thing to do. It brings different sets of people together and enhances understanding and mutual respect toward one another. While there are systemic challenges in execution, yet the outcomes far outweigh the degree of difficulty in implementation. Most importantly it helps in developing a symbiotic relationship between communities, which is important in the conflict management paradigm.

I am extremely happy to note that Brig Rajiv Williams, YSM, has covered a number of aspects, which bring about appropriate positioning of the Army in context to the civilian populace close by and in the process gets the willful license to independently operate under difficult situations, terrain and environment. I am also sure that the effort will help many varied segments of society to respect the good done for their community and am equally sure that the ethos with which the Armed forces undertake civic operations will be models of development amongst corporations and other entities in the domain of Corporate Social Responsibility.

Lt Gen Ranbir Singh (Retd)

Reflections on Corporate Social Responsibility (CSR) By Mrs Deepika Jindal, Chairperson Jindal Stainless Foundation

I am happy to note that Brig Rajiv Williams, former Group Head - CSR, Jindal Stainless Group, has penned down his thoughts on the relevance and importance of the sphere of corporate social responsibility. Over the last several years, CSR has become important for corporations, as supporting people to live a life of dignity and respect has a direct impact on business. Being an intrinsic part of business, whether as investors or customers, people inevitably grant corporations the 'license to operate'.

While the old business houses have always been agreeable to sharing their business profits for development, it had more to do with charity, welfare, and philanthropy. What was missing in this mix was the sustainability of business and the relationships built on the cornerstone of 'trust', which to a large extent is the focus of the new norm of CSR. It's this aspect that is well-articulated in the book well.

In my association with Brig Williams over the past 17 years, I have keenly observed how the projects have been developed since CSR became an important part of the Jindal Stainless journey, with the first baseline survey on the needs of communities having been carried out in 2008. As the Chairperson of Jindal Stainless Foundation, I am well-pleased with the result of our efforts. I can see how the communities in the remote parts of Odisha, Haryana, and Andhra Pradesh have changed their outlook towards business.

Our CSR activities focused on community needs and projects were initiated and sustained to take care of the people. It is extremely rewarding to see how the once uneducated women, who society inadvertently left out and left behind, have been encouraged to become entrepreneurs and bring about social change in their respective areas. Some have started their business with big buyers and been part of the supply chain of stores like Fabindia, Big Basket, and Mother Diary. As the famous Ghanaian scholar Dr James Emman Kwegyir Aggrey once said, "If you educate a man you simply educate an individual, but if you educate a woman, you educate a whole nation." It has been inspiring to witness this firsthand. I am glad that some stories of the journey towards empowerment so many have undertaken have been covered in the book.

It is also exciting to see how the farmers have benefitted through our CSR initiatives. Our success in grassroots programmes has led to government bodies becoming important stakeholders and partners in our work. A great example of this is how the complete agriculture extension services our CSR team innovatively rolled out have resulted in the Niti Aayog and other state governments taking note of the work we are carrying out, resulting in partnerships with the government. The sustainability pathway of our agriculture programmes was demonstrated during the two years of COVID-19, when technology was brought into procurement and supply chain management, making things more seamless for farmers. This innovation also came of service during the time of demonetization, when farmers were too cash-starved to buy seeds during the short window of time available to them, as their logistical hurdles are such that their crop has to be transported within a time frame, especially the perishable variety. All this was possible due to the CSR programmes, which focused on bringing technology to the farmers' doorsteps.

With such documentation endorsed in the book, I feel there are a number of lessons that can be drawn to give practical solutions to the communities being impacted by business. While inserts in the book have brought out Jindal Stainless Limited's CSR initiatives, which have been carried out by Jindal Stainless Foundation and other social entities through partnerships, I feel corporations need to come together and ramp up their efforts. We also need to support existing government infrastructure and projects and go to scale to see the greater vision of inclusive growth and development.

I hope this book serves as a great reminder of how a company's success should reflect in the areas surrounding its operations, and how it should trickle down to everyone in the vicinity. As corporates rise up, we need to make sure our countrymen rise up with them.

Deepika Jindal

Deepika Jindal
Chairperson Jindal Stainless Foundation

OP Jindal Group

Jindal Stainless Foundation
O.P. Jindal Marg,
Hisar - 125005,
Haryana, India

T: +91 124 449 4100
E: info@jindalstainless.com
W: www.jindalstainless.com

CHAPTER 1

Prologue

The Indian Army continues to carry out tasks beyond what just meets the eye of protecting the sovereignty of the country. Such tasks could well come under the purview of 'Beyond Military business activities'. These activities are those that come under 'aid to civil authorities' and include maintaining law and order, supporting the civil administration during natural calamities and other areas of engagement to facilitate in to bring an unwanted situation under control. All such 'beyond military activities' are formal official duties, which the military is required to fulfil as per the designated mandate, like saving lives during fire accidents or floods, conducting rescue missions and so on. All such tasks are the civil face of the military, but there are other tasks carried out by the Army, which do not strictly come under such category and can be classified under 'Army Social Responsibility' (ASR).

ASR and Corporate Social Responsibility(CSR) have a strong symbiotic relationship in our understanding of the development sector, in which disciplined social support leads to corporates getting engaged in community development, because both the institutions have 'people' at the 'centre' of all engagements. For it is the 'people' who are most important when we talk of development and growth and are the basis of the philosophy on which we should rely for security and business.

When I sought premature retirement from the Indian Army, after a very illustrious and rewarding career, I realized that it is the 'man' behind the 'machine', who has to be encouraged and motivated to ensure that he and his team put in their best towards goal accomplishment. After doffing my uniform, I started to dive deep into the relatively new concept being adopted in corporations and that was CSR based on the precepts of the triple bottom line – 'People, Planet, and Profit'. Again, the first 'P' was the critical mover and shaker for all that corporations have to focus on is to ensure they become sustainable entities. For it is the people who drive profits for the companies to survive and they, in turn, can survive only if corporations look after them, be it their employees, their local communities, or those in their supply chains. This first 'P' essentially focuses on the principle of 'respect'. The people focus remained intensely different areas of our deployment over the years in the Army. The support rendered in some areas was under different code names like 'Op Good Samaritan' or 'Op Sadbhavana.

As a young officer during the 1971 India-Pakistan war, and being from the infantry I was moved straight into the battle zone soon after graduating from the Indian Military Academy, Dehradun. Our training had to be cut short by five weeks and the excited young officers were sent to forward areas and into combat. It was a time of much transformation as we were now leading men into battle. Battle – yes, with an enemy whom we could identify and 'shoot to kill', the very basic tenet of our training at the military institution. What about the enemy, whom we could not identify or for that matter what about the civilians in the same area where enemy troops were deployed. They were just citizens – they were just people who by virtue of their abode had lived there for many years and did not have a direct role in any of the military-related activities. 'People', who were supposed to have been protected by the Pakistan military, a very important responsibility entrusted to it. However, when the Pakistan army failed to protect the locals as they retreated from the area it became a matter of great concern even for Indian Army troops as the Pakistani citizens had to be 'Cared for and protected' – a need far beyond Army responsibility in a conflict zone. I now write from the standpoint of the people who came in contact with my troops as we advanced into Pakistan in Shakhargarh area in what was then known as West Pakistan It was then that I realized 'People' are central to all endeavours of 'pride and prejudice' or in the space of 'conflict management'.

Before leaving the Indian Army, I had a rather fulfilling tenure at Drass, the coldest inhabited place in the world, in the Ladakh region of the State of Jammu and Kashmir. For it was soon after the Kargil war that the Army, as part of civil support, initiated 'Operation (Op) Sadbhavana' to look provide succour to the local population. In effect Op Sadbhavana came under border management and could well be considered an important adjunct of Army social responsibility towards people in the proximity of military cantonments and army posts. The concept itself was part of the larger agenda of 'conflict prevention' rather than being embroiled in 'conflict resolution' under the overall architecture of 'conflict management'. I will reflect upon the chasm that existed between the military and the civil before Op Sadbhavana, which resulted in the Kargil war. It is important for the military to have a good and harmonious relationship with civilians in the vicinity to ensure that the flow of information remains a key in the overall strategy of conflict management.

It was this realization and learning that encouraged me to join the development sector and get engaged in corporate social responsibility (CSR), around the time when it was becoming a buzzword in the country. The Army realized its social responsibility and how it helped in reducing terrorism in the area. On joining the corporate world as a development practitioner, I found a lot of similarity in engaging with the local communities by not following the earlier precepts of 'charity welfare philanthropy'(CWP), but adapting to the new model, which demands more inclusivity and value creation in geographies around factories and supply chains. The aim was to empower communities and, in the process, obtain the support of the locals, who in return provide the much required 'licence to operate'.

Military Individual Social Responsibility (MISR)

In addition to the ASR perspective mentioned above, the Directorate of Military Affairs, in June 2023, issued instructions to the three defence services relating to compulsory social service to be carried out by all personnel proceeding on leave. This in a way is to encourage and inculcate in troops the concept of 'Individual Social Responsibility' (ISR). Social activities that soldiers can carry out have been listed in the official instructions. Hence, it is a form of military individual social responsibility (MISR), which is part of a mandate and hence will be somewhat different to 'individual social responsibility,' which is more of volunteering and has a direct connect with the aspect of the 'joy of doing; the community good. This has a direct linkage with the 'head and heart' as it is not strictly on a project mode, which is a foundational principle of all corporate social responsibility initiatives. In addition, all the work done by soldiers needs to be documented and reports submitted to the units and formations up the chain on what activities have been carried out. That sure is a big task to ask from soldiers who need to enjoy their stay with their families after long periods of absence as they are posted in difficult areas with limited opportunities to keep their families in the stations of their postings, even in peace time locations.

Challenges around Mandatory Military Individual Social Responsibility

Forcibly making soldiers on leave carry out social work may lead to resentment and frustration. My rationale of such an observation is because all such community facilitation/work with society has to be performed from the heart. It has to be carried out with the intent of joyfully supporting a cause and that comes from within. Such forced activity by soldiers on leave have to be reported to the authorities with proper photographic evidence in support their claim, which, in turn, will give them some brownie points towards their official annual reports. This kind of a rat race will result in unnecessary challenges and result in peer pressure. Besides, it has also been reported that the efforts during the phase of such military individual social responsibility will promote government-sponsored schemes, which in a way alludes to endorsing all government activities, which may not be correct as an independent arm of the government machinery.

CHAPTER 2

Importance of Good Military-Civil Relations

Lesson from Kargil War

"Did you see those men on the top of the mountain?" An inquisitive shepherd asked his friend who had accompanied him for grazing his sheep on the slopes of Drass-Bhimbat area in the Kargil sector of Ladakh. "Why do you ask," Ghaffar asked young Shifat, who seemed scared as they ventured closer to the mountain top. "I just found them to be different from the rest of us in the area as they are much taller and broader and have a different dialect than the locals from this area."

This was a brief conversation of the two shepherds as they climbed the green meadows stretching from the lower reaches of their villages of Bhimbat and Drass to the heights of Marpola, Tololing and beyond. The reason for such a conversation was a sense of insecurity and unfamiliarity. Both Shifat and Ghaffar were regular visitors to the area, where they took their cattle for grazing. Such visits increased over the days and they found a larger presence of unfamiliar faces atop the mountains and on occasions the superlatives thrown at them were rather discomforting. Similar observations was made by some of their friends who also ventured out after hearing their tale. These men on top of the mountain were not from their villages nor were they from the villages nearby. Ghaffar on a serious note suggested to his friends that they need to inform the Army troops deployed at the base of the mountain and closer to their homes. The men seemed different and no one could understand their dialect. "Were they from Pakistan; they were surely not shepherds. Were they military personnel trying to peep into the areas dominating the Srinagar-Kargil road? Is there some kind of a threat to us," remarked Ghaffar. The six of them decided to inform the men in the local military garrison whom they had neither never ever met nor interacted with.

It was sheer determination and grit on the part of these grazers to enter the military cantonment and inform the soldiers of their having seen strange people atop the mountains. The military sentry at the gate to the camp shoed them away and warned them never to come anywhere close to the camp. The soldiers irritated with the locals for coming up with vague charges. The soldiers had been in the area for quite a while and had never seen such unfamiliar faces in the entire area.

Importance of breaking the Chasm between Civil and the Military in Conflict areas

It was this very disconnect between the Army troops deployed in the area and the civilians there that resulted in delayed action in confirming the information the boys brought. This led to the enemy soldiers taking advantage of the surprise element and massing a large troop deployment, which finally resulted in the Kargil war of 1999. I believe the conflict could have ended with less than the 528 deaths that were caused on the Indian Army. Such large a figure of casualties in uniform would surely have been avoided only if such a distinct chasm between the military and the civilians had not existed. The question of 'Civil -Military relations'.

When I analyze the 'why' of such discord, the only answer that comes to my mind is a distinct distance that was maintained between the two entities – the military and the civilians. It should well have been appreciated that the civilians were surely more familiar with the terrain and the environment. This major faux pas could perhaps have been overcome if the two had met and connected with each other and a form of social responsibility of the Army in the area of their deployment employed. It was a very important lesson that emerged after the conflict.

No more than a year after the limited Kargil war, I was posted as the commander of the brigade responsible for the areas where the conflict had taken place, that is Drass, Tiger Hill, Tololing, Bimbat, and Mushkoh, to name a few. Under a very able leadership of the senior commanders, a lot of emphasis was laid on building community relationships. The operation was named 'Op Sadbhavana', with the aim of helping the local communities through projects like skill development for the youth and women, education, women empowerment, improved nutrition, integrated health and so on. All such interventions were undertaken after ascertaining the needs of the communities after carrying out a kind of base line survey. The efforts focused on making the Army responsible for the very people the troops were deployed to protect and to safeguard Indian territory by ensuring the sanctity of the Line of Control (LoC) – that is, the border between India and Pakistan. With Kargil just over and the lesson learnt of the importance of closer relationships between the Army and civilians in the area, my entire formation, besides, carrying out our operational role was also engaged in supporting various types of projects for the community. The outcome of such projects was very heart-warming and profitable from the intelligence standpoint and the people became friends of the Army, who just a year earlier shunned their presence.

This was just a reflection of the Army's social responsibility, which was as important a task as being deployed along the border (LoC) and being exposed to all kinds of enemy fire from across it. The civilians became freer to communicate with the uniformed fraternity and share information not only of terrorists in hiding but also, through their local contacts, sharing information of enemy troops and terrorist group movement even before they infiltrated into the Indian side. I would think they in some form were acknowledging their satisfaction and hope in the Army's presence, which in civil parlance could in a way be termed as giving a 'licence to operate'.

Army Carrying Out Social Responsibility in a Remote Area

Against this backdrop, after doffing my military uniform, I thought of understanding how corporations acquiring land to build plants/factories in remote areas of the country will need to ensure good corporate-community connect for the latter to give corporations a 'licence to operate'. The challenges to such a format rested only on good corporate-community connect through activities which would give the communities an opportunity to live a respectable life. This was fundamental to good corporate governance through understanding societal needs and getting involved in corporate social responsibility (CSR) towards the target population at the bottom of the pyramid and supporting the overall development and inclusivity agenda for mutual interest and benefit. All this is important in the realm of branding and risk mitigation, besides an important parameter of investor interests and a favoured finance product.

CHAPTER 3

Understanding Army Social Responsibility

Army Social Responsibility (ASR) is a tool for improving community relations for it is the community in the vicinity of deployment that needs to be adapted in a manner that gives inherent security to the military deployed in their close proximity. However, this is not a rule and neither is it an exception. If intelligently applied, it can be a game changer and hence needs to be intelligently activated. There are a number of case studies, which merit the advantage of having civilians engage with the military in a holistic and dynamic manner rather than positioning them as mere cases of 'suspects'. For this very purpose, there are a number of operational projects like 'Op Samaritan' in the Northeast, 'Op Sadbhavana' in the erstwhile State of Jammu and Kashmir and similar humanitarian projects.

Army Carrying Out Rescue Mission after an Avalanche Struck a Village

'Operation Sadbhavana'/'Operation Good Samaritan'

A military civic responsibility combined with a focus on development. Development of the area and in the process the flora and fauna and, of course, better value creation. The start was on providing the local populace with quality education by establishing 'Goodwill schools'. It was though this facilitation on a partnership with the civil government (the likes of today's context of the PPP model) that proved to be a game changer. The people saw the benefit of such schools, where local teachers were hired and children's logistics and other admin needs met by the Army. The 'goodwill schools,' built on the existing infrastructure provided computer skills to the students, who at that time had little, if at all, any knowledge of the magic tool. Computers were given to them in adequate numbers. IT education and the midday meal programme further helped in providing the much needed nutrition and helped in improving student attendance.

It was a treat to see children from remote locations in Ladakh being taken to far-off places like Mumbai on educational tours. They even got an opportunity to meet and interact with the President of India at Rashtrapati Bhavan. Where would a child from such an area ever get a chance to visit the capital of the country and get an audience with the highest office of the country? The visits and tours were not an end by themselves. Returning to their villages, students, and teachers generated extremely infectious goodwill amongst the locals. The joy could be clearly seen on the faces of the village elders and others.

Encouraging locals to restore some of their local talents and culture as part of the Army's Sadbhavana program found favour amongst the people of Kargil and other locations. To name some such initiatives was the local sport of Drass – polo. This was a sport, which the locals loved but limited scope to indulge in it. As part of Sadbhavana, and commanding the brigade at Drass (the world's coldest inhabited place), I took this sport to the entire Ladakh region and organized inter-block and inter-district matches. Drass polo, as it was called, is played on ponies without stirrups – the riders rode their animals bare back. Despite precarious riding and with difficulty in manoeuvring, the players displayed strong grit and determination and excelled to such an extent that some of them were selected for teams to play outside the State.

Women empowerment was another major vertical in the Army's social responsibility paradigm, in which tailoring centres were opened. Women were also imparted training in various skills, especially those required for livelihood generation projects. This included sheep and goat rearing, shearing of wool, etc. The Army itself was a big market for the products made by local women, besides the requirements of local schools and other government institutions.

Similar projects on health care, environment protection and other community development projects to include self-governance programs found favour amongst the locals. This further encouraged government schemes to reach the needy and the Army helped the local district administrations to make government schemes available to the people.

These and many other programs for locals were supported by the Army and the youth were provided opportunities to achieve their dreams This also weaned them from the path of militancy and being recruited for subversive tasks. While the Army continued with its primary role of guarding the borders, yet it was important for it to look at the social side of its responsibility and thus the acronym 'ASR' – Army Social Responsibility gained importance.

Implications of Corporate CSR Funding Army Social Responsibility Projects

With the initial initiation of ASR through operations like Sadbhavana and Samaritan, the scope of corporations investing in such projects as part of their own CSR resulted in a dialogue between the Army and corporates. A number of corporations with a sense of déjà vu and pride started to park their mandatory CSR investments in military projects.

While there may be some good in getting that kind of funding support from corporations, yet according to Morgenthau's concept of 'power and politics' and, in the instant case, could relate to the concept of receiving 'aid', with obvious strings attached to a larger political agenda. Political realism has a distinctive approach and subject-matter. It stands for political standards for political actions and subordinates all other standards to it. Morgenthau emphasized the importance of the national interest, and in *Politics Among Nations* he wrote that "the main signpost that helps political realism to find its way through the landscape of international politics is the concept of interest defined in terms of power."

Hence, it is important for the Army to very succinctly analyze such support being rendered and seriously consider CSR funding from corporates. Should the Army encourage this kind of investment into the revenue model of social responsibility, which will include doling out funds/equipment to individuals regardless of whether they are war widows or battle casualties? Should the Army think of including corporations in funding infrastructure support for the two entities and others for whom the Army takes on the responsibility as per the norms of doing social good? These questions become real for the Army and opens up such opportunities for corporate CSR investments. It will be relevant to share inputs on such corporate CSR support being given to

Army projects during the past decade, especially after the mandatory law on CSR came into force in 2014, about which there will be some discussion in the subsequent paragraphs.

Many companies have taken up initiatives to support the physical and economic rehabilitation of soldiers who have been disabled in the line of duty. For example, Tata Motors, one of India's leading automobile manufacturers, has been actively involved in providing prosthetic limbs and wheelchairs to soldiers who have lost their limbs in the line of duty. Similarly, Reliance Industries Limited (RIL) has been providing financial assistance and job opportunities for disabled soldiers and their families through its CSR arm, Reliance Foundation.

Another area where CSR activities have made a significant impact is in the support of families of martyrs. Bharat Petroleum Corporation Limited (BPCL) has taken the initiative to provide financial assistance and educational support to the children of martyred soldiers. Similarly, the State Bank of India (SBI) has been providing financial assistance to families of martyred soldiers through its CSR arm, the SBI Foundation. It has contributed Rs. 2 crore to the Armed Forces Battle Casualties Welfare Fund (AFBCWF). The fund is extended to the armed forces for the welfare of the wounded in battle and to support dependents of personnel. The AFBCWF is a tri-service fund, which is utilized for grant of immediate financial assistance to families of soldiers/sailors/airmen who laid down their lives or were grievously injured in active military operations. The State Bank of India (SBI) has further donated a state-of-the-art advanced cardiac life support ambulance to the Army Hospital (Research & Referral), New Delhi, under its corporate social responsibility programme.

Wipro, IBM and TATA Consultancy Services have taken the

initiative to provide mental health support for soldiers. Tata Steel, Bharat Forge and Larsen & Toubro have set up veteran-friendly HR policies and training programs to help veterans re-enter the workforce. Saluting the exemplary grit and determination of Indian Army veterans, Hero MotoCorp, as part of their CSR initiative, handed over 125 Hero Destini scooters to disabled soldiers.

Infosys Foundation, the philanthropic and CSR arm of Infosys, has signed a memorandum of understanding (MoU) with the Directorate of Indian Army Veterans (DIAV) to provide educational grants and scholarships worth INR 30 crore to widows and children of army personnel, who have been impacted through physical casualty. Edtech company, Hero Vired, has entered into a new partnership with Text & Clicks Academy to upskil existing, retiring and retired armed forces personnel and veterans. This first-of-a-kind partnership offers training and placements in emerging technologies such as artificial intelligence, machine learning, and data science on a large scale. This collaboration aims to provide attractive employment opportunities that will allow Indian armed forces personnel to transit into corporate jobs with ease, creating alternate avenues for employment upon retirement.

The Indian Army, with CSR funding support from PETRONET LNG Limited (PLL), has collaborated to execute 'Project Kashmir Super 50', a programme aimed at improving the scholastic status of children from economically disadvantaged families in Kashmir. Hindustan Petroleum Corporation Ltd (HPCL) and the Indian Army are implementing a CSR project to coach and mentor less privileged girl students in Kargil. Spark Minda Foundation in collaboration with the Indian Army organized an 'Empowerment of People with Disabilities Camp' in Kupwara. The intervention covered more than 300 people affected by locomotive and speech and hearing disability.

Thoughts about Corporate CSR funds for Army Projects

It is in the above context that I suggest that the Army carry out introspection on such support being rendered by corporations towards social causes addressed by the Army. The bottom line of the assistance must not impact the independence of such goodwill and spread of social responsibility. It would encourage Army social responsibility to reach out to the remotest parts of the country, where the military is deployed and volunteers from corporations be encouraged to serve communities where projects need to be scaled up. Financial assistance for war widows, who are reasonable well supported through government schemes, should be avoided. However, employment opportunities for the widows and the differently-abled must be encouraged.

Funding Army goodwill projects from Corporate CSR, in the long run, will encourage infrastructure development and skill training around corporate manufacturing facilities/factories/ corporate institutions or similar projects. Environmental protection, WASH, health and hygiene projects and the like could well be developed through collaboration with industry.

CHAPTER 4

Informed Corporate Social Responsibility

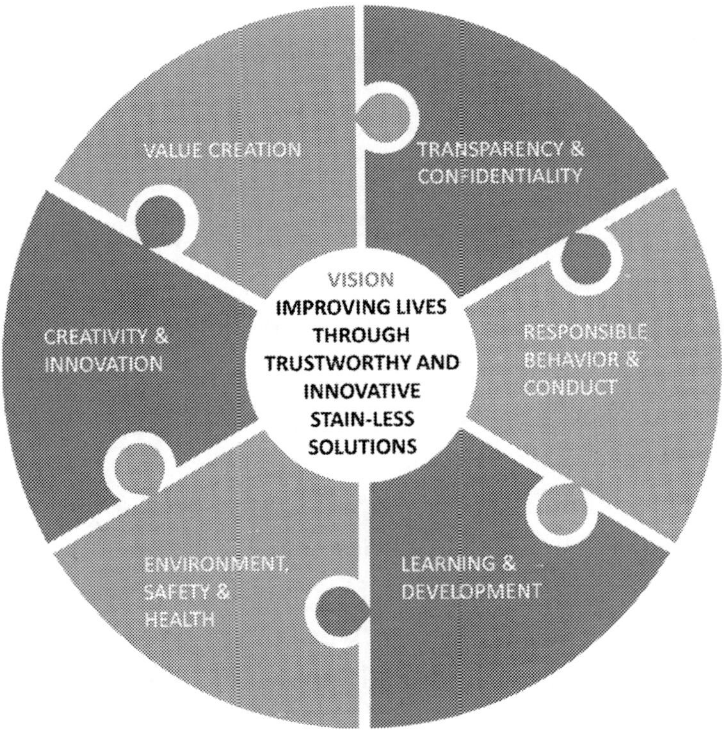

VISION & PRINCIPLES

What was familiar to all corporates was to feel good by doing good. Doing good from the surplus funds, which were put into a trust and the money spent (different from investing) on social causes. A kind of charity and donations. Building hospitals, schools, and usually with the name of the donor attached, a kind of branding was the norm of yesteryear. It was 'charity welfare philanthropy. Then why the sudden need to revisit the charity part of giving? Well I would think with the communities being more informed on their rights and the responsibilities of corporations in taking care of communities displaced when they set up their factories and plants, the demand for philanthropy became stronger. The people wanted to be part of the problem, which was created in the name of development. Inclusivity and shared value became apparent and the people wanted to be part of the process and growth.

Considering that corporations were moving into remote areas of the country to set up their manufacturing facilities, the question arose on who would run them. Will it always be the manpower moved from developed areas, which had the skill sets to operate the machinery set up to run the businesses. Would such migration create an imbalance in the spatial and demographic profile of the geography where corporations wanted to make their businesses successful? Would they merely plunder the natural resources from the natural owners of the land and merely give 'Caesar what belonged to him', that is, the government, as per the rehabilitation and resettlement (R&R) policies of the government, or would they have to engage with people on a format of 'beyond business responsibility;? It was the latter, when the corporates realized that merely sticking to the mandate as laid down by the local government, did not give them the 'licence to operate', which in turn makes it difficult for businesses to become profit centres. The realization further dawned on corporates that unless they took care of the 'people', the very purpose of their business, sustainable business cannot be assured.

It is from this precept that the triple bottom line (TBL) concept of business became important for corporations to adopt and make a success of their business. The 3 Ps of the TBL were 'People, Planet, and Profit', which relate to the three aspects of social, environmental, and economic factors of creating business value. Over the past five decades, environmentalists and social justice advocates have been struggling to evolve the concept of TBL into the public consciousness and monetize the social and environmental good created through investment made on various initiatives. This brought about a change in the philosophy of just the once familiar concept of charity welfare philanthropy' to corporate social responsibility, a 'beyond business responsibility' realization amongst corporations.

- *Strategic CSR is linked to a corporate leader's understanding of CSR*
- *CSR in today's context is an essential part of the business strategy*
- *CSR facilitates developing sustainable communities*
- *CSR is key to inclusive growth*

Strategic CSR

There are many examples on how such investments in social projects can bring about monetary changes in the communities benefitting from various initiatives. Besides investing in social projects, which have an impact on the environment, will have a direct monetary profit for a corporation. The TBL has to be measured in terms of how a corporation is investing in projects, which reduce the public investments in the health of the people or for that matter in employment accretion, etc. This helps in cost accounting processes and adds a brand value to the corporation carrying out such investments. Similarly, investments on natural capital and human capital also assist in measurement of the required TBL. Such are the international standards required for businesses to be recognized and markets improved across geographies. The social benefits in meaningful employment of disadvantaged citizens, and the reduction of society's welfare on disability costs, has a great value advantage to a corporate investing in such causes. All such investments contribute towards sustainability to business houses and further the branding, which is important for investors and markets.

It must also be appreciated that a large number of corporations, large, medium, and small, do not know how to invest their two per cent mandatory requirement on social projects in terms of design and implementation. Hence, they prefer to play safe and donate it to an institution, preferably a government institution having provisions to accept such donations under the mandatory CSR investment (as I prefer to call it, rather than what has been prescribed in the regulatory framework as 'spend'), and to play safe on the non-compliance part. As per the Companies Act 2013, all corporations have to invest 2 per cent of their profits as per the provisions below:

Companies Act Eligibility Criteria

"All companies registered in India, that have a net worth of Rs. 500 crore or more

or

a turnover of Rs. 1,000 crore or more

or

a profit of Rs. 5 crore or more in any one year;

are expected to spend 2 per cent of their profits in CSR w.e.f. April 1, 2014."

This is a large investment, which needs to be carefully planned and projects executed after a deliberate base line survey, which should bring out 'what people need and not what a corporate investing funds think that a community needs.' This is fundamental and based on the needs, which emerge, should programs and projects be initiated.

It must also be understood that funding the needs of projects have to be transparent and correctly reported on the site developed by the Ministry of Corporate Affairs, Government of India. The aim of such transparency is more to keep a check on the purpose of the funding as also a guideline for investing funds on projects as per designed schedules. It further helps in project monitoring and evaluation. The income of any fund or institution or trust as mentioned in the Income Tax Act of the Government of India and other details are given in various rules and regulations published by the Government of India from time to time. Hence, it is imperative for the company secretaries of corporations to keep themselves updated on the various rules and regulations as periodically amended to ensure that CSR projects are implemented either directly or through partner organisations in an appropriate and transparent manner.

CHAPTER 5

'Beyond Business Responsibility'

Corporate Social Responsibility (CSR) activities mandated for corporations to undertake have been articulated under Schedule VII of the Companies Act 2013. However, I am sceptical of the adjuncts attached with every activity, which portend to give a broad brush on the 'which all' engagements permissible under a particular activity listed as a CSR initiative. To put it into perspective I would like to flag one of the CSR activities mentioned in the Schedule, that is, 'poverty alleviation'. This activity has a large canvas of subsets, which need to be addressed, like supporting initiatives around social change, providing quality education, creating employment opportunities, giving a voice to women, environment protection, addressing issues around business, human rights, etc., There are similar amplifications expressed in the other activities mentioned. The bottom line of all such endeavours is to upgrade skill sets amongst various stakeholders so that they contribute towards growth and be a part of the Make in India campaign.

From the above, I would like to extrapolate that mandated CSR is no more a mere 'feel good' philanthropic initiative or that CSR can be clubbed under the much hyped 'compliance mode' as CSR was positioned earlier. Corporate CSR is reflective of undertaking missions 'beyond business', which is an important part in a corporation's survivability especially in the current context where a free and informed society has a direct impact on community relations making 'Corporate-Community-Connect' the critical mass of change.

We therefore need to look at various basic community requirements holistically and in keeping the related issues around CSR's triple bottom line approach, that is, People, Planet and Profit, with the first 'P', that is, i.e. 'People' as centric to all development. It is in this right connect that communities in close proximity to manufacturing and business facilities will give corporations a 'licence to operate' and hence corporations have to work towards focused community connect concepts. The bottom line of all CSR endeavours is to 'get it right' by carrying out a detailed analysis of community needs through a process of a base line survey before undertaking CSR initiatives in a defined geography.

It brings clarity that CSR is the strategic approach towards sustainable community development and the key to inclusive growth. With increased emphasis on sustainable economic development and the United Nation's defining Sustainable Development Goals, the importance of CSR engagement at the bottom of the pyramid (BOP) gains even more impetus. CSR interventions help employees to understand the community in the vicinity of their areas of responsibility and in the process addresses issues around 'business and human rights'. It is through such strategic CSR that corporations connect with people by firstly listening to them and then speaking the dialect most accepted by communities, that is, the dialect of *'language of the heart'* for businesses have a social consciousness and in that process have a responsibility toward the communities impacted by their business.

CHAPTER 6

The Indian CSR Journey

Indian industry has, over the years, been into charitable giving – sharing their wealth for goodwill essentially and subsequently for growth of the business. While there were exemptions from taxation in such donations, the intent remained at supporting communities. Over time, the act of just giving transformed into the act of social investment, when the concept of Gandhi's philosophy of 'trusteeship' found favour with many corporate leaders. However, with 'rights' issues picking up momentum with more informed societies, the benefits of community investments helped in finding solutions to various labour issues. The labour unions have a strong voice and are important stakeholders in a consultative process through the essentials of collective bargaining and freedom of expression. Such realization has dawned on corporate India as it has understood the benefits of dialogue and that has resulted in opinions in favour of corporations and the understanding on addressing community needs through community-led projects gave rise to Corporate Social Responsibility.

This gradual change brought CSR from the backroom to the board room. It changed from mere philanthropy to a more strategic approach and led towards sustainable businesses. Hence, CSR became a strategic tool for business houses and has become important to make businesses more community focused and sustainable.

Charity and philanthropy in yesteryears was more around establishing 'family trusts' and the goodwill factor was linked to religious sentiments. Gradually, this transcended into creating 'family foundations', which could implement various business-linked projects and welfare activities. Corporations realized that such giving was not only a good thing to do but a smart thing to ensure the growth of business as they found the advantage of 'licence to operate' with less disturbances forcing lockdowns at the manufacturing facilities and less agitations and strikes. The benefits led to business strategically designing projects which were sustainable and which directly helped businesses to grow.

It was at this stage that regulatory bodies were required to be set up and various policies framed to ensure the process became aligned to intent. The Department of Public Enterprises came up with CSR guidelines even before the national Voluntary Guidelines came into force, though essentially the public sector undertakings, which mandated PSUs to spend (not invest) on CSR projects between 3 and 5 per cent of their profits. These rules were then suggestive to bring about a change in the thinking of the private sector and the 'National Voluntary Guidelines' were formally released in 2009. This further brought about greater transparency in the system with a somewhat clear direction on how to go forward in the social sector space. The SEBI guidelines then mandated reporting, initially for the top 100 companies, then the top 500 companies and now it is the top 1,000 listed entities, based on market capitalization. The format is known as the business responsibility reporting (BRR) framework. Such efforts gave rise to other international reporting standards like the GRI and incorporating OECD guidelines into reporting frameworks. In addition, the global CSR and sustainability policies, like that of the UN Global Compact, the UN Guiding Principles on Human

Rights, the ILO declaration, the Accountability AA1000 standards, the SA 8000 standards, the ISO 26000, the SROI Network framework and other policies became more relevant.

With an excellent sustainable economic development framework in place, the industry must leverage the social good factor by promoting various community-based projects and further employee volunteering programs, which will establish a link with the work force and the community who are part of the product supply chain. This gives the employees and the management an opportunity to get connected with each other as also with their target audience, Whoever is the target of engagement, the bottom line in the realm of CSR is to engage and connect with people and link them with the threads of 'head and heart' by speaking '*the language of the heart and making them a party in all development through a community-based participatory approach.*'

Investment in CSR

Since the introduction of the Act and in conformity with the mandatory requirement for corporations to spend on CSR, from a modest approximately Rs. 8,000 to 10,000 crore spent in the first year of the Act, that is, during FY 2014-2015, the collective annual amount spent by private corporations in 2019 was approximately Rs. 25,000 crore and in FY 2021-2022, the investment touched close to Rs. 27,000 crore. Although this is an important milestone achieved by making CSR investment mandatory, yet it is a small amount when compared with the government spends on CSR as per government data available for the financial year 2021-2022 which stands tall at over Rs. 300,000 crore.

My perception on the above topic of spending on CSR is neither just about the colossal fund spent on CSR projects nor is it to do with the scale of the supposed beneficiaries but is to do 'how' the investment has taken place with the component of accountability attached. I feel the latter and not only about the project investment and just filling up a survey form with a whole lot of tick marks against various boxes, but it is to do with community connect and getting them to own projects. I am of the opinion that it is about the quality of projects rather than the quantity reported. Most corporations opt to bench mark the numbers of lives impacted but I feel differently about the whole thing about numbers and prefer an impacted community, a cheerful community, an empowered community. It is more satisfying for the community to speak rather than corporations' tom-tomming their own achievements. I say this with conviction because had the numbers reported as beneficiaries impacted truly, the government and private sector investment on social projects would have some symbiotic relationship with a visible impact.

Collaborations

- Identify and re-work on CSR projects to ensure dynamism
- More thrust on SDG 17: Collaborations
- Work on innovative strategies that are mutually beneficial and rewarding

For the past decade plus there have been conversations around the public-private-partnership (PPP) model, obviously centric to the additional fourth P – 'People' added some years later. After all, projects being worked out are for improving the lives of 'People' and hence the fourth 'P' should have been the first in the model recommended. Notwithstanding what I have stated, such partnerships are essential and must be encouraged. The government, which is responsible to provide basic amenities and protection to people and industry and are key stakeholders in all development agenda, need to be supported by the private sector on a collaborative model. The existing structures should be further strengthened rather than create parallel structures thereby duplicating the designed efforts and making the whole exercise unnecessarily competitive.

It is equally important to establish collaborative models amongst private sectors co-located in the same geography or having similar business activities across the country. While private-private partnerships and collaborations may be complex management issues, they must be encouraged. There are obvious reasons for such an observation since most corporations want the CSR engagement to become a business case from their standpoint and ask a question on what benefits will accrue by such collaboration. However, I am convinced that with a deep understanding of the overall social development and with the prime aim of improving the lives of people, the industry collaborative model is very much doable and must be encouraged through the platform of industry associations and local governments.

CSR and MSMEs/MNCs

Since the enactment of the Companies Act 2013, the MSME sector has been constrained on investing funds on CSR projects as mandated in the provisions of the Act. With a large number of MSMEs having profits of over Rs. 5 crore, they are required to invest in CSR and that is a challenge with most of the MSMEs since they neither have the expertise nor the experience in community engagement. Hence, the correct utilization of funds, which may vary from under a lakh to several lakh, the spend piece does become challenging. However, over time, there is a better understanding and more MSME companies have started implementing projects through partnerships with NGOs and other agencies and this will have a major impact on local communities.

A number of multinational companies such as Starbucks, The Body Shop and Microsoft have establish well-developed codes of conduct; they also strive to achieve some social missions in order to do business ethically, minimize negative environmental impacts, raise public attention on certain issues, raise funds and donations, increase employees' job satisfaction, and more. It is important to study some key takeaways from the way CSR is being carried out across the world by IT giants like Apple and Microsoft.

MNCs, including their holding companies or subsidiaries operating in India as defined in Section 2 (Clause 42) of the Indian Companies Act 2013, and having branch offices in India and if they fulfil the criteria specified in Section 135(i) of the Act, then they are mandated to comply with the provisions of Section 135 of the Act and the rules published thereafter. With such a clause, it is clear that all foreign companies in India and who qualify under the clause mentioned have to spend or invest 2 per cent of their profits in CSR projects. Presently, there are over 1,000 foreign companies operating in India and hence their investments will amount to a substantial increase. It must also be appreciated that Indian MSME entities will soon be seeking greater collaboration with foreign companies and try and support the Atmanirbhar effort. However they have to develop requisite expertise in meeting international manufacturing standards and that by implication would mean ensuring quality in input material, training capacity, ethical conduct, and so on. It is these qualities, which will remain key in moving towards the direction of a self-reliant India.

Atmanirbhar Bharat – Make in India

Self-reliant India, as I see it, has always been the vision of the country since Independence, but progress has been slow with perhaps inadequate funds available to lay greater emphasis on strengthening manufacturing processes within the country. The climate has since changed and whether it was demonstrated with the IT capabilities of the tech giants or the MSMEs in the electronic space or the infrastructure firsts with the establishment of quality infrastructure development, the bottom line of such a direction has been linked to fund availability and 'political will'.

It is being over-ambitious to think that this will happen very quickly as some processes take long to fructify after meeting various standards and undergoing time-tested trials. This becomes very relevant and important in the area of defence and allied security network abilities. While we have the large PSUs and large private Indian corporations investing much on R&D, yet there are technologies imported to ensure a quality benchmarked at international standards and that will take time and patience. We need to accept such recourse and aim for building capacities of the work force. Hence, corporations have to use funds in this direction to make India Atmanirbhar and work on projects with a 'Make in India' tab. Much of the work can be carried out by the

MSME sector, which provides components to large corporations and CSR funds can be optimally utilized in such an effort.

Business and Human Rights

While activities, which can be undertaken under CSR as per the Act, do not mention human rights or activities connected with it, yet if we break down the components linked to various defined activities, business and human rights become central to all engagement, whether it has to do with education, health, women's empowerment, environment or skill building. All have a direct impact on human rights. The United Nations Guiding Principles (UNGP) have clearly articulated that businesses have to work towards the second pillar of the UNGP, that is 'Respect'. This by itself is all encompassing and will facilitate business operations by respecting the work force, respecting communities, the environment and all other related attributes. This will give businesses the much-needed 'licence to operate' and create a healthy business environment. Hence, corporate houses need to build on this aspect and understand how CSR can contribute to building good relations through the important pillar of 'Respect'.

The first pillar enunciated in the UNGP is that of 'Protect', the responsibility of the State that is to protect the interest of people, institutions, industry and the like. While much is happening in this field, yet much is still desired. This was adequately measured with the recent happenings seen during the current trying pandemic time. We saw the gaps in the protect segment during the initial period of reverse migration. – How the people were cared for and uncared for in equal measure. The government along with the corporations through their CSR funds supported the reverse migration process, yet far too many inadequacies were noticed. The follow-up of the migrants in terms of giving them employment at their place of origin needs to be followed up with adequate resolve and fervour.

Migration/Reverse Migration and CSR

As mentioned above, there was a large exodus of migrant workers as they returned to their homes and villages. This had a lot to do with the human rights part and related to both the pillars of 'Protect' and 'Respect'. However, we need to ensure that schemes of the government be implemented and reach the target population. It will be prudent to mention that although the Centre has developed schemes to provide free food to an estimated number of 80 million undocumented migrant workers, yet from reports available, no more than 20 million of the population benefitted from the scheme. This is primarily because of the 800,000 tonnes of rations earmarked for the 80 million migrants at a scale of five kg food grains a month to be given free could not be lifted by the States. There are grave challenges in implementation with a weak delivery system of States and their capacities. Other issues relating to having ration cards to access the public distribution system, etc., further make it difficult for the beneficiaries, firstly to be identified and secondly to be supported. Similar complexities are experienced in providing employment to the masses even under the MNRGS scheme, where the migrant workers do not have job cards.

The corporations need to engage with communities and through their CSR must provide support to the government agencies and reduce the gap between the two. There is an absolute necessity to strengthen the agriculture base in the villages. While the government is trying to make agriculture a key area of job creation, yet without the support of corporate expertise and more joining this segment of intervention, the task continues to be difficult and time consuming. Collaborations can be worked out in the space of providing loans to small farmers and creating post-harvest agriculture infrastructure. It must be understood that a large quantity of food, vegetables and fruits go waste due to lack of such infrastructure.

CHAPTER 7

CSR and Sustainable Business Strategies

Sustainability and CSR are the foundational principles of growth, development, and good business, which contribute towards United Nations SDGs. Although essential, I believe that CSR laws in India should not be limited to being a compliance issue through government legislation but should, more importantly, be an integral part of a corporation's business ethics and business responsibility. The Companies Act 2013 is prescriptive in many ways on how CSR initiatives should be implemented and clearly spells out how corporations need to spend on CSR.

CSR and Sustainable Growth

CSR, by definition, has a lot to do with the 'Triple Bottom Line' accounting framework, which incorporates three dimensions of performance: Social, environmental and financial, commonly referred to as the 3Ps – 'People, Planet, and Profit'. When we dive deep into the rudiments of engagement, the 'Social' aspect remains central in the sustainable development agenda, because the other 2Ps – 'Planet' and 'Profit'– have a direct impact on the first 'P' – People.

I firmly believed at Jindal Stainless Limited (JSL), where I started CSR that it is all about a continuing commitment to behave ethically and contribute towards overall economic growth by improving lives of the workforce, their families, communities, and societies at large. Projects are implemented either directly or through the company's Foundation in collaboration with other implementing partners and are enablers of sustainable community development. Through its initiatives, the company creates an environment by providing opportunities to its employees to connect with each other and with the community at large. It aims to provide a platform that empowers the community through need-based programs, making beneficiaries self-reliant through a process of direct intervention. The company focuses on going 'Beyond Business Responsibilities' stressing on the importance of seeing a change in the lives of communities around its plant locations as well as in other geographies. Some of the key focus areas are education and skill training with a strong focus on self-reliance and entrepreneurship development, women's empowerment, and integrated health care with specific focus on eradication of disease from a specific target area. It has also been engaged in the program on agriculture extension by providing a direct connect between a farmer and the buyer and has been addressing the issue of environment and, in the process, of reducing carbon emissions.

While most projects mentioned above have a common strategy for implementation, yet there are natural calamities, which necessitate a different approach and methodology. For example, there were some projects, which had to be tweaked during the de-monetization phase and of course when the SARS pandemic hit the country, with a prolonged period of lockdown and so on. While the projects continued in a scaled down manner, yet the activities continued because of the element of being sustainable. After the situation improved, the projects bounced back and revived over a relatively short period of time. Some of the challenges faced in implementation of select CSR projects initiated by JSL have been highlighted in the subsequent paragraphs.

Challenges Faced in Implementation of select CSR Projects Initiated by JSL

The challenges faced when Corporate Social Responsibility was being started in JSL essentially stemmed from the understanding of the concept by the senior leadership. The spend on CSR activities had to be understood as investment in CSR projects having long-term benefits, likely to be seen after a few years of that investment and certainly not seen as an immediate outcome. Once they understood that such projects helped communities in mitigating challenges caused by the company due to various difficulties faced by the people like land acquisition, environmental degradation and even changing the entire psyche of people ousted from their hearths. It was only when such realization dawned upon them and they understood the long-term gains of such investment with 'People' at the bottom of the pyramid being impacted by their operations and that it was that segment of the society that will provide the corporations not only the required 'licence to operate' but also be the market of tomorrow, that the same leadership understood the worth of such investments.

Hence, to overcome that major challenge from within the organisation, it is very important to first address the promoters of business houses and then adopt the 'top down' approach to ensure that CSR projects are good for the sustainability of the corporation as also for business. Such an approach leads to several other challenges like thematic areas and the investment to be made on activities as also finding the right implementation partners to undertake the work.

KEY CSR PROJECTS

Corporate

JSL Flagship CSR Project: 'Krishi Unnati'

The agriculture extension project thorough its implementing partner, Gram Unnati Foundation, embarked upon a project to double farmers' income. The innovative project was designed quite differently and focused on providing end to end solutions to farmers and make agriculture an attractive investment. The aim of the project is also to stymie and reduce migration by providing the local communities with opportunities close to their abode.

While the project had gained favour with the NITI Aayog and other state governments, it actually proved worth the investment during the de-monetization and pandemic periods. Some of the major problems encountered during the post-demonetization phase were the availability of liquid cash for transportation of harvested crops. Since the backward integration with digitalization of payments was already in place, farmers who had joined the project did not face many difficulties in money transfers.

There was a different set of challenges faced by farmers during the pandemic phase, when a strict lockdown was imposed in 2020-2022. Some of the major problems faced were about providing markets for harvested crops with limited, or in some cases, no labour available, limited logistics and marketing support, lack of pesticides, fungicides, seeds for planting during the kharif crop plantation season, limited time period available for such planting, etc. To mitigate the problem, close integration with the state governments especially with the states of Odisha, Haryana, UP, MP and Uttarakhand, helped in combating the problems. In the process, the Gram Unnati Foundation, our implementing partner, was given a licence to procure directly from farmers and mitigate their distress sales.

Similar activities were worked around the only 'aspirational district' of Nuh in Haryana, where collating essential data of farmers affected is important for the government to provide support. It is an extremely important exercise to ensure farmers tide over the present crisis and address the issue of livelihood. Incidentally, the Government of India has designated 126 poorest districts in the country as aspirational districts. The challenges of agriculture supply chains across the country required innovative solutions, especially with most agriculture processors or retailers including new online players who did not have backward integrated supply chains that enable them to purchase agriculture produce from the source. It was a difficult period for famers who were finding themselves in a difficult position with limited buyers especially with a number of agriculture processors being forced to cease operations or operate at a lower capacity due to raw material supply constraints.

Jindal Stainless CSR, along with Gram Unnati Foundation and Four Leaf Cover, has been working directly with farmers for over seven years to source agricultural produce at terms more favourable than those offered by the traditional mandi-based systems and together built a technology-enabled model that enables procurement directly from farmers and sell to institutional buyers without middlemen. This enabled the project to unlock value within the supply chain for the benefit of farmers. The relationship between the implementing agency and over 500,000 farmers across six states built on trust and respect has made the project sustainable and profitable.

- The Agriculture extension project, Krishi Unnati, is one of our flagship CSR projects
- The intent of this initiative is to mitigate the problems faced by farmers especially during the post demonetization period as also the current pandemic phase

Sustainable Agriculture

During the early lockdown period, JSL along with Gram Unnati Foundation collaborated with the Delhi Government to provide fresh vegetables to community kitchens. The source of such support was local farmers around Delhi/NCR, who were starved for markets and suddenly found the opportunity attractive. Such quick steps across states for farmers urgently requiring agricultural inputs, massive outreach campaigns with partners like Bayer Crop Sciences were held for the partners to understand the needs of farmers. Working with local district administrations, it was important to establish a connect between them and the farmers especially with regard to planning and organizing the required stocks inventory and delivering inputs at farmers' doorsteps in safe and sanitized conditions.

Equally important was to develop a web application, which would help demand data collection for a particular commodity, for example, fresh vegetables in select colonies, where the demand was high and should be aligned to the availability index. Such measures helped in better and timely access to items like fresh vegetables at affordable rates and at the same time ensured that farmers have a ready market for their produce. Through such an arrangement, which may be short and intense, yet it ensured that consumers and producers were connected directly while traditional supply chains were disrupted.

The other major problem, especially during the pandemic, which was faced by farmers, was when the crop was ready to be harvested there was very scarce or no labour available to cut the standing crop. There were also other problems like logistical support, marketing support, availability of pesticides, fungicides, and availability of seeds for planting for the next kharif crop season. In addition, the limited time window that was available for such planting, etc., added to the challenges. While some of these challenges have since been addressed, solutions to other issues are still being worked out to ensure farmers do not suffer due to the prevailing conditions.

JSL has been engaged with both the governments of Odisha and Haryana as also with some other States with relevant Memorandum of Understanding in place to support farmers. JSL's implementation partner, Gram Unnati Foundation was given a licence to procure directly from farmers and mitigate their distress sale problems and understand the needs of farmers urgently requiring agricultural inputs. Major outreach campaigns with Bayer Crop Sciences had to be initiated. Working with the local district administrations, we even delivered inputs at the farmers' doorsteps in safe and sanitized conditions. Additionally, during the early lockdown stage, we teamed up with the Delhi Urban Shelter Improvement Board to supply fresh vegetables daily to community kitchens serving food to the most affected by the lockdown. This gave an assurance to the farmers of a safe and assured supply chain during the critical phase of the pandemic.

Women's Empowerment and Livelihood Generation

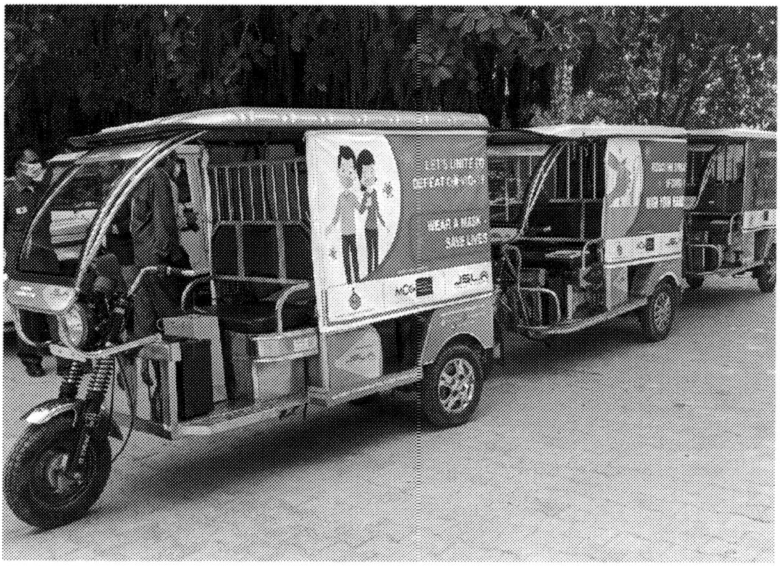

JSL has undertaken a number of initiatives on livelihood generation and women's empowerment with the aim of entrepreneurship development. The projects undertaken include creating self-help groups and providing various activities for capacity building from activities linked projects, to sourcing and marketing initiatives. Training has been organized for women in rural areas to divert them from the usual badi, papad, pickle, jam and chutney making and encouraging them towards setting boutiques and salons. They have also been trained in dress designing and fashion technology and finance management.

JINDAL STAINLESS FOUNDATION:
IMPROVING LIVES

Hole-in-the-

Infrastructure and community development

Integrated Health Care

Producer Company Board of Directors meeting

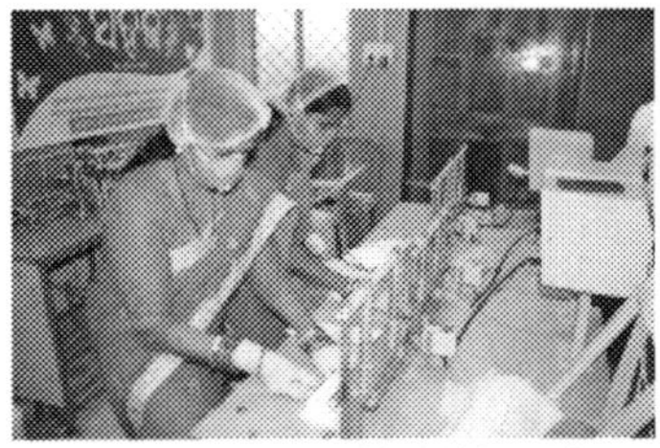

SAHAJ Sanitary Napkin Making Unit

- Capacity building of artisans through various design workshops
- Development of new product as per the domestic and international market needs
- Establishing the marketing channels for the handmade Golden Grass products

Golden Grass Project

Mushroom Cultivation

Beetle vine Cultivation

At JSL, CSR activities are taken as opportunities to give back to society in every way possible. JSL's various CSR projects mainly include:

(a) Education and vocational training
(b) Integrated health care
(c) Women's empowerment and entrepreneurship development through self-help groups (SHGs). Asmita and Sahaja are major projects focussed on women's empowerment.
(d) Preservation of art and culture
(e) Business and human rights
(f) Rural development

Women Trained in Stainless Steel Fabrication

Disha Project

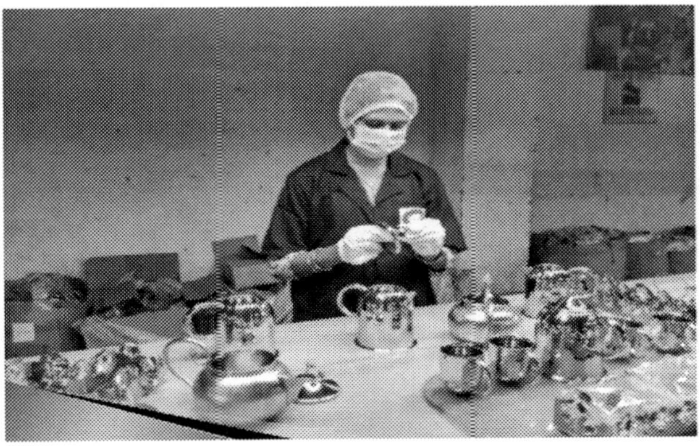

Disha Project: Rohad

In addition to empowering women in the urban rural areas in states like Haryana and Odisha, JSL, in partnership with Xynteo, a Norwegian organisation, and the UNDP, has empowered women to work in the stainless steel sector by imparting training to them in cutting, welding, quality control and marketing of stainless steel products. In the area of training imparted to women in steel making and moulding, there were challenges on getting candidates, especially from Haryana, who though keen, were being restrained by the menfolk and restricted to their homes. However, following frequent visits to homes of the trainees by mobilization teams, the families got involved in understanding the benefits in the opportunity and the visits had a positive impact on the community which had once objected to their women going out of their homes for training. These women were later drivers of the program. This was a major intervention as it truly displayed the instincts of empowered women leading to an empowered community in a rather conservative society. Over time, it has been observed that with women working alongside their male colleagues in the stainless steel factory, production has increased, quality checks carried out by women controllers has led to almost negligible product rejects and has impacted the company's bottom line positively. Such a joint effort has impacted the working ethos and work environment with the initial hesitation observed amongst the male colleagues of having women work alongside them to encouraging them to further their skills and improve their chances of promotions. This has been a major game changer in the empowerment process.

Some of the outcomes of our initiatives have been women setting up their own enterprises. In fact, they have gone a step further in collaborating with other SHGs engaged in either making by-products required for adding value and with groups under a mutual agreement for marketing on a profit sharing model. To amplify such an effort, there are SHGs that source, grade and package pulses, rice, gram, etc. and supply to SHGs making products and the chain is established, which leads to the process of forward and backward linkages.

Some of the other initiatives include setting up production units to make safety jackets, home linen products, etc. Collaboratively, the SHGs have even established a production unit registered under the brand name 'Asmita,' another flagship CSR project of JSL. The production unit has established a number of satellite Asmita centres, which support the main centre.

ASMITA Project

ASMITA Project

As part of its women's empowerment programme, JSL, with the support of an NGO, has established a production unit for local women. It basically aims at nurturing skills for home furnishing products and apparel like school uniforms among women. The projects have attracted many international and national brands which include Fab India, Good Earth and many more. Many schools in the nearby areas chose ASMITA for placing orders for their school uniforms. Not only school uniform, ASMITA also major production of safety jackets which is customized and sold according to the demand of the customers. Their major customers for safety jackets are local industries that include TATA Steel, Jindal Stainless and many other manufacturing companies in Odisha and other states.

Women have achieved social and economic status after being involved in SHGs. The institution is a tool that helps in community participation for rural women's development and encourages them to get involved in entrepreneurships activities. ASMITA has not only made them economically independent but has also instilled confidence in them. Women are not only using their money to become independent but also to support their families, thus becoming a strong backbone for the family financially. Women are conscious to travel in Jaipur, Orissa, due to lack of public transport and safety. It was observed during the research that the major reason for women to join ASMITA was to financially support their families and partially become financially independent. Another major reason to join ASMITA was to enhance their skill.

Sahaja Project

The Sahaja Project was started with a small number of women from remote parts of Odisha, who were trained in making sanitary napkins. The social good from such an intervention had a great impact on the local community and the outcome was visible from a number of perspectives. Firstly, the women of the project encouraged other women from the villages, especially adolescent girls, to adopt healthy hygiene practices and improve the overall village health indices. Secondly from a low income generating activity, the women's group started marketing the product in schools and other villages and increased its earnings many times over. Sahaja entrepreneurs went in for getting their logo certified and their product registered as a small industrial activity under the DIC and obtained further registration as an MSME. While Jindal Stainless Group supported the initiative and strengthened the SHGs, it was the entrepreneurship spirit that made the production unit profitable and branded.

Aligning CSR Projects with UN Sustainable Development Goals (SDGs)

Besides the above, JSL has been factoring various areas of SDGs in all its programmatic engagements. With its new initiative of mapping the projects aligned with SDGs through a technology-based platform, a very clear and robust system with requisite monitoring processes have ensured a pathway that shows promise for the future. It is equally important to mention that various SDGs have different approaches of reporting and documentation. For example, SDGs need to focus on the impact on social and environmental projects using real time data analytics, generate data stories and create brand engagement as also do automate project level monitoring through an evidence-based approach. As per our experience, it is important for us to work on a two-step SDG mapping exercise down to target indicator level as per the UNDP guidelines.

JSL intervention could be included under SDGs 1, 2, 3, 4, 6, 11 and 17, besides some other SDGs, where the process of M & E is underway. Poverty alleviation is addressed through interventions of providing food for the poor and migrant workers, especially during the COVID-19 crisis. This has been mapped under the indicator of 1. 5. 1. Similarly, SDG 2 has been addressed though our farmer intervention projects in partnership with Gram Unnati Foundation (GUF) and Claro Energy and both activities have been mapped under SDG 1 indicators 2.3.1 and 2.3.2.

- Installation of water kiosks at various locations including Rohad, Pathredi, Hisar and Jajpur
- Installation of solar water pump for irrigation purpose

Rural Development Initiatives

Theme: Plastic Pollution, Water Conservation, Waste Management, Air Pollution

Theme: Sports & Fitness

SDG 3, which deals with integrated health care, has been adequately addressed through partners like Roko Cancer, besides other projects around health interventions through the indicator 3.4.1 and so on. The education indicators 4.1 and 4.5.1 where ITES education and providing quality education to the differently-abled, especially the hearing impaired is being imparted though our partner NDS and the data is well captured. The UN SDG 6, that is, clean drinking water, is also directly linked with health SDG 2. This project is being implemented by our partners, Piramal Foundation and Swajal. It is also important to note that the menstrual hygiene project with Sachi Saheli is a component of the WASH project and is included under the same SDG.

The environment impact and sustainable cities linked to SDG 11 have benefitted communities in a positive manner as recorded under indicators 11. 7. 1 and 11. 2. 3. The partnership for developing parks rests with Prabhav Foundation and through their intervention, the local self-government wants to take the project to other locations in the State of Haryana. You will acknowledge that the partnerships listed above adequately lend toward SDG 17.

Carbon Mitigation Strategies

In addition to undertaking sustainable CSR projects and tree plantation drives, water mitigation strategies to include water harvesting, engaging with farmers in climate resilient agri-practices, sustainable park initiatives and so on, JSL has also been engaged in reducing its carbon footprints. This has been a huge investment as we worked on climate adaptive technologies and investment in high technology manufacturing processes. These are expensive practices and do require support from various agencies to include the Government. While the developing countries are working towards creation of funding mechanisms to support such initiatives, yet in our region not much effort is being made towards this very important area to support corporations.

Hence, it is important to bring all projects under the Sustainable Development Goals and map the outcomes through the prism of the UN's 171 indicators. It is in such alignment that the way forward based on data can help in accomplishment of a select pathway of growth and development. While I have addressed only some of the areas being undertaken by JSL Group, yet I am certain the combined efforts of all corporations through technology will bring out a clear picture of where we are and how we are going towards the national agenda of reporting SDGs with data each year.

JSL has taken various initiatives under energy efficient projects and process optimization.

JSL is certified with ISO 50001:2018 standards which indicate JSL's commitment towards energy efficiency.

Some of the Projects undertaken by JSL for the reduction of carbon footprint during financial year 2019-20 were as follows:

(a) Energy conservation through various high-end energy efficiency processes accrued a saving of approximately 6,500 tonnes of CO_2 reduction.

(b) Fuel conservation processes – like waste heat recovery boilers, coke oven gas, which was flared in the open earlier has now completely stopped by installation of gas purification units. Direct charging of liquid ferro chrome in electric arc furnaces, up-gradation of LED lights and import of clean energy to the tune of 18,986 Mwh and so on.

(c) Additional steps towards regular energy and water audits as also regular replacement of old systems is a continuous ongoing process.

(d) Biofuel and CPP boilers being blended with coal-fired boilers.

Special Projects Focused Around COVID-19

JSL, through its Foundation, initiated action to combat COVID-19 even before the formal letter was issued by the Ministry of Corporate Affairs with regard to the 'Clarification on investing CSR funds for COVID-19'. We started work supporting migrant and daily wage workers in Delhi/NCR and the communication of 23 March 2020 helped us expand the scope of our response in mitigating some of the problems of the marginalized sections of society during the current 'lockdown' phase.

The initial planning started and stages planned on the phases perceived was based on assessed needs to combat the problem.

Areas of Interventions

As perceived, there were essentially five ways of providing support during the initial phase of combating COVID-19:

- ***Awareness:*** Awareness amongst communities regarding safe practices
- ***Medical institutions:*** Provision of equipment and resources to medical institutions to develop a more resilient healthcare system
- ***Health workers:*** Supporting frontline workers and community members with materials and supplies
- ***Vulnerable Sections of Society:*** Support vulnerable sections who have no income source to avoid financial stress and

improve access to food and essential resources

- ***Research Organizations:*** Expedite research on identifying testing techniques, vaccines and cures to expedite recovery through medical advancements.

Phases

- ***Preparatory Phase:*** Awareness
- ***Anticipated Migration Phase:*** Food (dry rations and prepared food support
- ***Long-term Phase:***
  - Support medical institutions
  - Support communities by linking above support with livelihood
  - Assistive digital technology in the area of telemedicine and consultation
  - Supporting vulnerable sections, with no stable incomes, by improved access to food and essential resources

We offered food, medical, and sanitation supplies to migrants and daily wage workers during the lockdown period, and also to families in several places, including Delhi-NCR and our neighbouring communities in our plant locations – Hisar (Haryana) and Jajpur (Odisha). Additionally, we provided food to affected communities through community kitchens run by the Delhi Government and NGOs. We also arranged for buses to ferry migrant workers to their homes in other parts of Uttar Pradesh.

Despite the government's ardent efforts, the pandemic had affected nearly 80 per cent and 54 per cent jobs in urban and rural economies, respectively, (according to Indian Society of Labour Economics). At the same time, an alarming gap in healthcare infrastructure had been observed during the pandemic. Healthcare and upskilling, especially in rural India, are areas demanding immediate attention. Support for innovation and technology development will make healthcare infrastructure robust and affordable. Similarly, focus on upskilling masses will help youth earn better opportunities and livelihoods.

Impactful CSR Tools

CSR has to be linked to the business strategy with a clear statement of purpose and with the intent of leading companies for the benefit of all stakeholders, that is, customers, employees, suppliers, communities and shareholders. It also would imply the act of being inclusive in operations, with little impact on the environment and ensuring proper waste management methodologies, etc.

Analyse community needs in details and see how you can address the issues in a collaborative manner, making them the first responders and ensuring their stakes in an intervention are in proportionate measure. In some cases, they can also become shareholders in a project-linked investment with responsible positions of secretary and treasurer of the group created from among the community. Such inclusivity will help in making a sure success of a project as the outcome will directly impact beneficiaries from the community. The ease of engagement will also be relevant to help towards project sustainability. Equally important is to focus on assets and strengths of the community as they can be used to improve community lifestyles. Hence, identify the needs and resources of communities.

Therefore, the community assets by definition could well be a resource person, a physical structure like a school, a hospital, a community centre, a library or even a social club. Such resources will be of great assistance in project delivery. The strengths of community service, public transportation, early education and community re-cycling facilities as also culture centres might connect with people. Hence, to feel there is an absolute lack of everything when carrying out need assessment will be a fallacy and optimal utilization of the available resources will be missing. Always remember that everyone has skills and talents and all can provide useful knowledge about the community and their links to people they know will help in the overall project implementation strategy.

Employee volunteering will be a great way of program ownership of the company. People take pride in owning a project and that leads to accountability and further growth and development with an inert sense of satisfaction. Research shows that shared leadership and employee empowerment have a number of benefits, including increased team effectiveness, a stronger sense of community, improved employee perception management, higher levels of employee satisfaction and greater corporate loyalty.

While branding is a different subset of communication, yet it is important for the CSR strategy not to be exclusive and secret. It is important to share the genuine work being carried out with external stakeholders as it fosters enthusiasm and increases stakeholder engagement and accountability. Include various communication tools like website, social media, newsletters, email up dates, reports and so on. Sharing such interventions generates interest in CSR engagements and indicates transparency and the accountability factor.

Branding CSR

As per my understanding, CSR branding is really a new norm, where corporations engaged in CSR activities want the stakeholders to know that the corporations are engaged in social work beyond business. The Government too is inclined to roll out programs with a tagline promoting the initiative as a Government program and maybe projecting an image of a person leading the initiative. However, from an egoistic outlook and perhaps for branding purposes, the question needs to be understood through the lens of short-term gains as also from the standpoint of a long-term social impact. Branding must also be intelligently applied from an ethical standpoint as it could be perceived as an unjust projection, which will draw flak across geographies.

When we dive deep into the issues of branding, I feel it is important for the beneficiaries to know as to who is supporting the initiative through display of activity boards and hoardings but only in the specific area of intervention. From recent trends it is observed that corporations go to town to showcase 'The What' of the supposed 'Good' is being done by them by projections across locations and through different platforms of social spaces. Corporations should be rather subtle in such presentations and in fact I would recommend that the beneficiaries themselves should be the brand ambassadors and share important outcomes of the support rendered to them. It was because of the investment in the project that the beneficiaries see the change in their lives as also in the lives of the local community.

CHAPTER 8

Individual Social Responsibility

I often quiz myself why have we forgotten our childhood learning, when our parents and teachers insisted on the "Do it yourself (DIY)" concept. Get up early, make your own bed, put off the light and fan (for the few who could afford it) and close the tap when you have done your toilet. Ensure that the tap does not run when you brush your teeth. The focus was on conservation and discipline. Why have those practices, which were well ingrained in us, have since been forgotten and we fail in our responsibilities as 'Now parents' to instruct our children. Are we too busy or is it just that we can afford to pay what is to be paid for as excessive use.

Replenishing our closets with 'the new', when the old still looks new has become a fashion and encourages us to make it a point to prove a point that I have since added 'more' to our already more. A party conversation, which percolates down to gen next to boast and feel elated, when some pseudos who consider them friends make you feel special as you flaunt your wealth or façade of wealth. It is time for each one to reflect and see what can be done to disengage ourselves from short-term pleasures and instead prepare to be a caring lot of citizens. Let us go back to the basics and share the joy, which rightly needs to be spread by engaging with friends and family as the family values, which have been taught to us in childhood and just in case we have missed the goodness of restraint, then let us acquire and pass it on to our children, who hopefully will pick up the good and pass it on to their progeny. It is an interesting awakening and the earlier we realize its importance the more beneficial it will be for humanity.

In relationship to the environment, the Individual Social Responsibility (ISR) collective will have a great impact. 'Each one – Teach one', in a thematic conduct like garbage segregation and cleanliness should be the mantra for each child and for each person. The child is the father of man, the often heard saying, is the reason that I mentioned, because they are really the movers and shakers of tomorrow. They are the ones who will make their parents realize the importance of such an education. Hence in a way it is an individual, who once encouraged, can encourage others to follow an unwritten set of rules.

When we carry out an impact analysis of the collective savings by these little interventions, there is very strong data to support the good created in such effort. By switching off lights and using just what is necessary and regulating ACs on when the ambient temperature may require a 25 degrees Celsius control, rather than pegging the temperature a few notches below. Saving – saving and saving of electricity will help in the larger picture of reducing levels of pollution and in turn help in mitigating the problem of climate change. Similar areas of environment preservation like tree plantation and water, when carried out by individuals for individuals, help in a joyful beginning.

Hence, ISR is a very important way of addressing climate-related issues and helping a nation-state in becoming more responsible. A classic example is Japan, where it is difficult to find trash on the roadside and where children make a point to keep their areas clean and green. Such measures make us responsible and it is not only the big picture, which we need to worry about, but the small home type of responsibilities, which will add to support the big picture.

Impact Assessment and Reporting

It is important for corporations to carry out a third party impact assessment of their CSR projects periodically as it gives them a line of thinking on how and what should be taken forward. The Social Return on Investment (SROI) format is a great tool, which gives a corporation a feel good factor or otherwise and helps in carrying out a mid-course correction.

However, what is not reported is not done. Hence, it is equally important to ensure that the findings are reported as per the designed standard formats. Such a reporting process gives more credibility to the 'act' and hence increases the marketability of a corporation. The international reporting standards are good international markets and need to be followed as per the Indian context. The BRR and other Indian standards have been developed after a very strong consultative process and remain an ongoing activity for the future.

Measuring CSR performance should include how the information is collected and from whom it is collected. This will help in assessing the data with a certain amount of accuracy and proper sharing of data collected.

CHAPTER 9

The Environment, Social and Governance Framework

The Environment, Social and Governance (ESG) Framework refers to various activities which take place in a company on the non-financial aspects of a company's operations that can have a direct impact on its long-term financial performance and sustainability. While the 'E' refers to the impact of a company on the environment, the 'S' relates to all social impacts of the company on society at large and the 'G' is the company's internal governance structure, which impacts the long-term goals of an organization. The ESG considerations have been gaining importance as stakeholders, including investors and customers, place increasing importance on responsible and sustainable business practices and hence they have a direct relationship with the company's priorities in investments.

This has increased in recent years due to several reasons like financial performance, risk management, sustainable business practices, etc., as also the need to comply with Government regulations and practices. The aspects of financial performance have to be viewed through the lens of short-term and long-term investments. All stakeholders in today's context view the company's performance on the ESG matrix. The ESG risks, such as climate change and human rights violations, can pose significant threats to a company's operations and financial performance.

Once realization dawns amongst the corporations then they have to formulate ESG strategies, which, in turn, will help them in improved decision making after identifying and managing the risks attached because of their acts of omission. All these aspects have a direct impact on the Board's accountability and further improves the branding of the corporation.

CSR and ESG

Corporate Social Responsibility (CSR) and Environment, Social, and Governance (ESG) are related but distinct concepts in the realm of corporate sustainability and responsible business practices. CSR typically focuses on a company's voluntary actions and initiatives to address social and environmental issues, often beyond legal requirements. It encompasses philanthropy, community engagement, sustainability efforts, and ethical business practices. ESG, on the other hand, is a broader framework that evaluates a company's performance and behaviour across three key dimensions: environmental, social, and governance and ESG factors are considered in investment decision-making to assess a company's long-term sustainability and risk profile. CSR initiatives can vary widely and may include activities such as charitable donations, employee volunteer programs, environmental conservation projects, and ethical sourcing practices. ESG factors on the other hand are more standardized and typically include specific metrics related to environmental impact (e.g., carbon emissions, water usage), social aspects (e.g., labour practices, diversity and inclusion), and governance practices (e.g., board diversity, executive compensation, transparency).

Under 'Integration into Business Strategy', CSR initiatives are often seen as separate from core business operations and may be driven primarily by ethical considerations, reputation management, or stakeholder expectations, whereas ESG factors are increasingly integrated into the overall business strategies and decision-making processes of companies. They are viewed as material to financial performance and long-term value creation, influencing investment decisions, risk management, and operational efficiency.

The 'Measurement and Reporting' aspect is equally important and different from each other. CSR activities are typically evaluated through qualitative measures, such as community impact assessments, employee satisfaction surveys, and stakeholder engagement feedback while ESG on the other hand focuses more on performance measured using quantitative and qualitative indicators, often through standardized frameworks and reporting guidelines (e.g., Global Reporting Initiative, Sustainability Accounting Standards Board). This allows for comparability and benchmarking across companies and industries. Hence to highlight the differences, I would once again state that CSR and ESG both emphasize different aspects of corporate responsibility and sustainability. While CSR tends to encompass a broader range of voluntary initiatives and stakeholder engagement efforts, ESG provides a structured framework for evaluating and integrating 'Environmental, Social, and Governance' factors into business practices and investment decisions.

Concluding Thoughts

Army Social Responsibility in the context of Corporate Social Responsibility has come to stay as major sustainable military and business tools. The various tenets of the concept have to be understood in a holistic and altruistic manner, without the motif of any personal gains. It is only when ASR and CSR projects are implemented either exclusively or in collaboration, with the intent of community benefit, that the effort will find positivity in the investment. Like any other project, there are challenges attached to be successful while undertaking a social project; however unless we make an effort towards achieving the desired goals and objectives and with a firm commitment, nothing will come out of the effort except a limited impact on making the environment more secure and society more inclusive and developed.

Alignment and collaborations are the only way to scale as far as CSR is concerned as corporations with limited budgets when compared with government reach and extent, need to develop partnerships with mutual adoration. We must respect communities and that can only happen once we respect ourselves and our own ilk. Hence, compliance or compulsions should not be drivers of our CSR initiatives; instead, we must have clarity of focus and touch all stakeholders responsible to have a symbiotic relationship for co-existence and mutual benefit.

The future of Corporate Social Responsibility (CSR) is likely to continue evolving in response to societal and environmental challenges. Businesses are increasingly recognizing the importance of sustainability, ethical practices, and social impact in their operations. Key trends shaping the future of CSR are integration of CSR into the core business strategy as they realise that social and environmental responsibility can drive innovation, enhance brand reputation, and create long-term value and the need to focus on environmental sustainability. With growing concerns about climate change and environmental degradation, CSR efforts are placing greater emphasis on reducing carbon footprints, conserving resources, and adopting renewable energy sources; hence the emphasis on social impact and expanding beyond traditional philanthropy.

It is in this context that CSR has been engaged in winning the hearts and minds of the local communities, especially the manufacturing and extractive industries around their plant locations and in the process continue to serve the local communities through the projects mentioned earlier like poverty alleviation, education, healthcare access, and diversity and inclusion. It is equally important to carry out the roles in a more transparent manner enforcing the factor of accountability in all their CSR practices. This includes transparent reporting on environmental, social, and governance (ESG) metrics and demonstrating tangible progress toward sustainability goals. Emphasis is also being now given to advancements in technology and taking steps to take into account certain measures linked to block chain, artificial intelligence and big data analytics. These technologies enable better tracking of supply chains, monitoring of environmental impacts, and identification of social issues. The importance of SDG 17 on 'Collaboration and partnerships' cannot be compromised as corporations to go to scale in their CSR efforts have to collaborate with governments, non-profit organizations and other stakeholders to address complex social and environmental challenges. These partnerships can amplify the impact of CSR initiatives and drive systemic change. Overall, the future of CSR is likely to involve a continued shift towards more holistic and impactful approaches that prioritize sustainability, social responsibility, and ethical business practices.

APPENDICES

Highlights/Extracts of Important Government of India Notification

Appendix 1

Ministry of Corporate Affairs Notification, New Delhi, 22 January 2021

रजिस्ट्री सं. डी.एल.- 33004/99 REGD. No. D. L.-33004/99

भारत का राजपत्र
The Gazette of India

सी.जी.-डी.एल.-अ.-22012021-224640
CG-DL-E-22012021-224640

असाधारण
EXTRAORDINARY

भाग II—खण्ड 3—उप-खण्ड (i)
PART II—Section 3—Sub-section (i)

प्राधिकार से प्रकाशित
PUBLISHED BY AUTHORITY

सं. 31] नई दिल्ली, शुक्रवार, जनवरी 22, 2021/माघ 2, 1942
No. 31] NEW DELHI, FRIDAY, JANUARY 22, 2021/MAGHA 2, 1942

कारपोरेट कार्य मंत्रालय

अधिसूचना

नई दिल्ली, 22 जनवरी, 2021

सा.का.नि. 40(अ).— केन्द्रीय सरकार, कंपनी अधिनियम, 2013 (2013 का 18) की धारा 135 और धारा 469 की उपधारा (1) और उपधारा (2) के द्वारा प्रदत्त शक्तियों का प्रयोग करते हुए, कंपनी (कारपोरेट सामाजिक दायित्व नीति) नियम, 2014 का और संशोधन करने के लिए निम्नलिखित और नियम बनाती है, अर्थात्:-

1. **संक्षिप्त नाम और प्रारंभ.**- (1) इन नियमों का संक्षिप्त नाम कंपनी (कारपोरेट सामाजिक दायित्व नीति) संशोधन नियम, 2021 है।

(2) ये राजपत्र में, जब तक इस अधिसूचना में स्पष्टतया अन्यथा उपबंध न किए गए हों, इसके प्रकाशन की तारीख को प्रवृत्त होंगे।

2. कंपनी (कारपोरेट सामाजिक दायित्व नीति) नियम, 2014 में नियम 2 के स्थान पर निम्नलिखित नियम रखा जाएगा, अर्थात्:-

"**2. परिभाषाएं** – (1) इन नियमों में, जब तक कि संदर्भ से अन्यथा अपेक्षित न हो,-

(क) "अधिनियम" से कंपनी अधिनियम, 2013 (2013 का 18) अभिप्रेत है;

G.S.R. 40(E).—In exercise of the powers conferred by section 135 and sub-sections (1) and (2) of section 469 of the Companies Act, 2013 (18 of 2013), the Central Government hereby makes the following rules further to amend the Companies (Corporate Social Responsibility Policy) Rules, 2014, namely:

1. Short title and commencement. - (1) These rules may be called the **Companies (Corporate Social Responsibility Policy) Amendment Rules, 2021.**

(2) They shall come into force on the date of their publication in the Official Gazette unless explicitly provided elsewhere in this notification.

In the **Companies (Corporate Social Responsibility Policy) Rules, 2014** (hereinafter referred to as the said rules), for rule 2, the following rule shall be substituted, namely:

"**2. Definitions.** - (1) In these rules, unless the context otherwise requires,-

(a) "Act" means the Companies Act, 2013 (18 of 2013);

(b) "Administrative overheads" means the expenses incurred by the company for 'general management and administration' of Corporate Social Responsibility functions in the company but shall not include the expenses directly incurred for the designing, implementation, monitoring, and evaluation of a particular Corporate Social Responsibility project or programme;

(c) "Annexure" means the Annexure appended to these rules;

(d) "Corporate Social Responsibility (CSR)" means the activities undertaken by a Company in pursuance of its statutory obligation laid down in section 135 of the Act in accordance with the provisions contained in these rules, but shall not include the following, namely:

(i) activities undertaken in pursuance of normal course of business of the company:

Provided that any company engaged in research and development activity of new vaccine, drugs and medical devices in their normal course of business may undertake research and development activity of new vaccine, drugs and medical devices related to COVID-19 for financial years 2020-21, 2021-22, 2022-23 subject to the conditions that -

(a) such research and development activities shall be carried out in collaboration with any of the institutes or organisations mentioned in item (ix) of Schedule VII to the Act;

(b) details of such activity shall be disclosed separately in the annual report on CSR included in the Board's Report;

(ii) any activity undertaken by the company outside India except for training of Indian sports personnel representing any State or Union Territory at national level or India at international level;

(iii) contribution of any amount directly or indirectly to any political party under section 182 of the Act;

(iv) activities benefitting employees of the company as defined in clause (k) of section 2 of the Code on Wages, 2019 (29 of 2019);

(v) activities supported by the companies on sponsorship basis for deriving marketing benefits for its products or services;

(vi) activities carried out for fulfilment of any other statutory obligations under any law in force in India;

(e) "CSR Committee" means the Corporate Social Responsibility Committee of the Board referred to in section 135 of the Act;

(f) "CSR Policy" means a statement containing the approach and direction given by the board of a company, taking into account the recommendations of its CSR Committee, and includes guiding principles for selection, implementation and monitoring of activities as well as formulation of the annual action plan;

(g) "International Organisation" means an organisation notified by the Central Government as an international organisation under section 3 of the United Nations (Privileges and Immunities) Act, 1947 (46 of 1947), to which the provisions of the Schedule to the said Act apply;

(h) "Net profit" means the net profit of a company as per its financial statement prepared in accordance with the applicable provisions of the Act, but shall not include the following, namely:

(i) any profit arising from any overseas branch or branches of the company, whether operated as a separate company or otherwise; and

(ii) any dividend received from other companies in India, which are covered under and complying with the provisions of section 135 of the Act:

Provided that in case of a foreign company covered under these rules, net profit means the net profit of such company as per profit and loss account prepared in terms of clause (a) of sub-section (1) of section 381, read with section 198 of the Act;

(i) "Ongoing Project" means a multi-year project undertaken by a Company in fulfilment of its CSR obligation having timelines not exceeding three years excluding the financial year in which it was commenced, and shall include such project that was initially not approved as a multi-year project but whose duration has been extended beyond one year by the board based on reasonable justification;

(j) "Public Authority" means 'Public Authority' as defined in clause (h) of section 2 of the Right to Information Act, 2005 (22 of 2005);

(k) "section" means a section of the Act.

(2) Words and expressions used and not defined in these rules but defined in the Act shall have the same meanings respectively assigned to them in the Act."

3. In the said rules, in rule 3, in sub-rule (2), in clause (b), for the words, brackets and figure "sub-section (2) to (5)", the words, brackets and figure "sub-section (2) to (6)" shall be substituted.

4. In the said rules, for rule 4, the following rule shall be substituted, namely:-

"**4. CSR Implementation.** – (1) The Board shall ensure that the CSR activities are undertaken by the company itself or through -

(a) a company established under section 8 of the Act, or a registered public trust or a registered society, registered under sections 12A and 80 G of the Income Tax Act, 1961 (43 of 1961), established by the company, either singly or along with any other company, or

(b) a company established under section 8 of the Act or a registered trust or a registered society, established by the Central Government or State Government; or

(c) any entity established under an Act of Parliament or a State legislature; or

(d) a company established under section 8 of the Act, or a registered public trust or a registered society, registered under section 12A and 80G of the Income Tax Act, 1961, and having an established track record of at least three years in undertaking similar activities.

(2) (a) Every entity, covered under sub-rule (1), who intends to undertake any CSR activity, shall register itself with the Central Government by filing the form CSR-1 electronically with the Registrar, with effect from the 01st day of April 2021:

Provided that the provisions of this sub-rule shall not affect the CSR projects or programmes approved prior to the 01st day of April 2021.

(b) Form CSR-1 shall be signed and submitted electronically by the entity and shall be verified digitally by a Chartered Accountant in practice or a Company Secretary in practice or a Cost Accountant in practice.

(c) On the submission of the Form, CSR-1, on the portal, a unique CSR Registration Number shall be generated by the system automatically.

(3) A company may engage international organisations for designing, monitoring and evaluation of the CSR projects or

programmes as per its CSR policy as well as for capacity building of their own personnel for CSR.

(4) A company may also collaborate with other companies for undertaking projects or programmes or CSR activities in such a manner that the CSR committees of respective companies are in a position to report separately on such projects or programmes in accordance with these rules.

(5) The Board of a company shall satisfy itself that the funds so disbursed have been utilised for the purposes and in the manner as approved by it and the Chief Financial Officer or the person responsible for financial management shall certify to the effect.

(6) In case of an ongoing project, the Board of a Company shall monitor the implementation of the project with reference to the approved timelines and year-wise allocation and shall be competent to make modifications, if any, for smooth implementation of the project within the overall permissible time period.".

5. In the said rules, in rule 5, for sub-rule (2), the following sub-rule shall be substituted, namely:-

"(2) The CSR Committee shall formulate and recommend to the Board, an annual action plan in pursuance of its CSR policy, which shall include the following, namely:-

(a) the list of CSR projects or programmes that are approved to be undertaken in areas or subjects specified in Schedule VII of the Act;

(b) the manner of execution of such projects or programmes as specified in sub-rule (1) of rule 4;

(c) the modalities of utilisation of funds and implementation schedules for the projects or programmes;

(d) monitoring and reporting mechanism for the projects or programmes; and

(e) details of need and impact assessment, if any, for the projects undertaken by the company:

Provided that the Board may alter such plan at any time during the financial year, as per the recommendation of its CSR Committee, based on the reasonable justification to that effect."

6. In the said rules, rule 6 shall be omitted.

7. In the said rules, for rule 7, the following rule shall be substituted, namely:-

"7 **CSR Expenditure.** - (1) The board shall ensure that the administrative overheads shall not exceed five per cent of total CSR expenditure of the company for the financial year.

(2) Any surplus arising out of the CSR activities shall not form part of the business profit of a company and shall be ploughed back into the same project or shall be transferred to the Unspent CSR Account and spent in pursuance of CSR policy and annual action plan of the company or transfer such surplus amount to a Fund specified in Schedule VII, within a period of six months of the expiry of the financial year.

(3) Where a company spends an amount in excess of requirement provided under sub-section (5) of section 135 , such excess amount may be set off against the requirement to spend under sub-section (5) of section 135 up to immediate succeeding three financial years subject to the conditions that –

(i) the excess amount available for set off shall not include the surplus arising out of the CSR activities, if any, in pursuance of sub-rule (2) of this rule.

(ii) the Board of the company shall pass a resolution to that effect.

(4) The CSR amount may be spent by a company for creation or acquisition of a capital asset, which shall be held by -

(a) a company established under section 8 of the Act, or a Registered Public Trust or Registered Society, having charitable objects and CSR Registration Number under sub-rule (2) of rule 4; or

(b) beneficiaries of the said CSR project, in the form of self-help groups, collectives, entities; or

(c) a public authority:

Provided that any capital asset created by a company prior to the commencement of the Companies (Corporate Social Responsibility Policy) Amendment Rules, 2021, shall within a period of one hundred and eighty days from such commencement comply with the requirement of this rule, which may be extended by a further period of not more than ninety days with the approval of the Board based on reasonable justification.".

8. In the said rules, for rule 8, the following rule shall be substituted, namely:-

"**8. CSR Reporting.** - (1) The Board's Report of a company covered under these rules pertaining to any financial year shall include an annual report on CSR containing particulars specified in Annexure I or Annexure II, as applicable.

(2) In case of a foreign company, the balance sheet filed under clause (b) of sub-section (1) of section 381 of the Act, shall contain an annual report on CSR containing particulars specified in Annexure I or Annexure II, as applicable.

(3) (a) Every company having average CSR obligation of ten crore rupees or more in pursuance of sub-section (5) of section 135 of the Act, in the three immediately preceding financial years, shall undertake impact assessment, through an independent agency, of their CSR projects having outlays of one crore rupees or more, and which have been completed not less than one year before undertaking the impact study.

(b) The impact assessment reports shall be placed before the Board and shall be annexed to the annual report on CSR.

(c) A Company undertaking impact assessment may book the expenditure towards Corporate Social Responsibility for that financial year, which shall not exceed five per cent of the total CSR expenditure for that financial year or fifty lakh rupees, whichever is less."

9. In the said rules, for rule 9, the following rules shall be substituted, namely:-

"**9. Display of CSR activities on its website.** - The Board of Directors of the Company shall mandatorily disclose the composition of the CSR Committee, and CSR Policy and Projects approved by the Board on their website, if any, for public access.

10. Transfer of unspent CSR amount. - Until a fund is specified in Schedule VII for the purposes of sub-section (5) and (6) of section 135 of the Act, the unspent CSR amount, if any, shall be transferred by the company to any fund included in schedule VII of the Act.".

10. In the said rules,-

(i) The Annexure shall be numbered as "Annexure –I" and in the heading of Annexure I as so numbered, after the words "BOARD'S REPORT", the words and figures "FOR FINANCIAL YEAR COMMENCED PRIOR TO 1ST DAY OF APRIL, 2020" shall be inserted;

(ii) after Annexure–I as so numbered, the following Annexure shall be inserted, namely:

"ANNEXURE II

Format for the Annual Report on CSR Activities to be Included in the Board's Report for Financial Year Commencing on or After 1st Day of April, 2020

1. Brief outline on CSR Policy of the Company.

2. Composition of CSR Committee:

Sl. No.	Name of Director	Designation/ Nature of Directorship	Number of meetings of CSR Committee held during the year	Number of meetings of CSR Committee attended during the year
1				
2				
3				

3. Provide the web-link where Composition of CSR committee, CSR Policy and CSR projects approved by the board are disclosed on the website of the company.

4. Provide the details of Impact assessment of CSR projects carried out in pursuance of sub-rule (3) of rule 8 of the Companies (Corporate Social Responsibility Policy) Rules, 2014, if applicable (attach the report).

   Details of the amount available for set off in pursuance of sub-rule (3) of rule 7 of the Companies (Corporate

5. Social Responsibility Policy) Rules, 2014 and amount required for set off for the financial year, if any

Sl. No.	Financial Year	Amount available for set-off from preceding financial years (in Rs)	Amount required to be set-off for the financial year, if any (in Rs)
1			
2			
3			
TOTAL			

6. Average net profit of the company as per section 135(5).

7. (a) Two per cent of average net profit of the company as per section 135(5).

   (b) Surplus arising out of the CSR projects or programmes or activities of the previous financial years.

   (c) Amount required to be set-off for the financial year, if any

   (d) Total CSR obligation for the financial year (7a+7b-7c).

8. (a) CSR amount spent or unspent for the financial year:

Total Amount Spent for the Financial Year (in Rs.)	Amount Unspent (in Rs.)				
	Total Amount transferred to Unspent CSR Account as per section 135(6)		Amount transferred to any fund specified under Schedule VII as per second proviso to section 135(5)		
	Amount.	Date of transfer.	Name of the Fund.	Amount.	Date of transfer.

(b) Details of CSR amount spent against **ongoing projects** for the financial year:

(1)	(2)	(3)	(4)	(5)		(6)	(7)	(8)	(9)	(10)	(11)	
Sl. No.	Name of the Project.	Item from the list of activities in Schedule VII to the Act.	Local area (Yes/No).	Location of the project.		Project duration.	Amount allocated for the project (in Rs.).	Amount spent in the current financial Year (in Rs.).	Amount transferred to Unspent CSR Account for the project as per Section 135(6) (in Rs.).	Mode of Imple-mentation Direct (Yes/No).	Mode of Implementation - through Implementing Agency	
				State.	District.						Name	CSR Registration number.
1.												
2.												
3.												
	TOTAL											

(c) Details of CSR amount spent against **other than ongoing projects** for the financial year:

(1)	(2)	(3)	(4)	(5)		(6)	(7)	(8)	
Sl. No.	Name of the Project	Item from the list of activities in schedule VII to the Act.	Local area (Yes/No).	Location of the project.		Amount spent for the project (in Rs.).	Mode of implementation - Direct (Yes/No).	Mode of implementation - through implementing agency.	
				State.	District.			Name.	CSR registration number.
1									
2									
3									
	TOTAL								

(d) Amount spent in Administrative Overheads

(e) Amount spent on Impact Assessment, if applicable

(f) Total amount spent for the Financial Year (8b+8c+8d+8e)

(g) Excess amount for set off, if any

Sl. No.	Particulars	Amount (in Rs.)
(i)	Two per cent of average net profit of the company as per section 135(5).	
(ii)	Total amount spent in the financial year	
(iii)	Excess amount spent in the financial year [(ii)-(i)]	
(iv)	Surplus arising out of CSR projects or programmes or activities of the previous financial years, if any	
(v)	Amount available for set off in succeeding financial years [(iii)-(iv)]	

9. (a) Details of Unspent CSR amount for the preceding three financial years:

Sl. No.	Preceding Financial Year.	Amount transferred to Unspent CSR Account under section 135 (6) (in Rs.)	Amount spent in the reporting Financial Year (in Rs.).	Amount transferred to any fund specified under Schedule VII as per section 135(6), if any.			Amount remaining to be spent in succeeding financial years. (in Rs.)
				Name of the Fund	Amount (in Rs.)	Date of Transfer.	
1.							
2.							
3.							
	Total						

(b) Details of CSR amount spent in the financial year for **ongoing projects** of the preceding financial year(s):

(1)	(2)	(3)	(4)	(5)	(6)	(7)	(8)	(9)
Sl. No.	Project ID.	Name of the Project.	Financial Year in which the project was commenced.	Project duration.	Total amount allocated for the project (in Rs.).	Amount spent on the project in the reporting Financial Year (in Rs).	Cumulative amount spent at the end of reporting Financial Year (in Rs.).	Status of the project - Completed/ Ongoing.
1.								
2.								
3.								
	Total							

10. In case of creation or acquisition of capital assets, furnish the details relating to the asset so created or acquired through CSR spent in the financial year

    (asset-wise details).

    (a) Date of creation or acquisition of the capital asset(s).

    (b) Amount of CSR spent for creation or acquisition of capital assets.

    (c) Details of the entity or public authority or beneficiary under whose name such capital asset is registered, their address, etc.

    (d) Provide details of the capital asset(s) created or acquired (including complete address and location of the capital asset).

11. Specify the reason(s), if the company has failed to spend two per cent of the average net profit as per section 135(5).

Sd/-	Sd/-	Sd/-
(Chief Executive Officer or Managing Director or Director).	(Chairman CSR Committee).	[Person specified under clause (d) of sub-section (1) of section 380 of the Act] (Wherever applicable).

APPENDIX 2

General Circular No. 14 /2021

E-file No. CSR-05/01/2021-CSR-MCA
Government of India
Ministry of Corporate Affairs

5th Floor, 'A' Wing
Shastri Bhawan, Dr. R.P. Road
New Delhi-110001.

Dated: 25th August 2021

To,
All Regional Director,
All Registrar of Companies,
All Stakeholders.

Subject: Frequently Asked Questions (FAQs) on Corporate Social Responsibility (CSR) -reg.

Madam/Sir(s),

The broad framework of CSR has been provided in Section 135 of the Companies Act, 2013 (**herein after referred as 'the Act'**), Schedule VII of the Act and Companies (CSR Policy) Rules, 2014 (**herein after referred as 'the CSR Rules'**). Further, Ministry had also issued clarifications including FAQs from time to time on various issues concerning CSR.

2. A number of significant developments have taken place since then. The Ministry has notified the amendments in Section 135 of the Act as well in the CSR Rules on 22nd January 2021 with an aim to strengthen the CSR ecosystem, by improving disclosures and by simplifying compliances. In response to such amendments, Ministry has received several references and representations from stakeholders seeking clarifications on the various issues related to CSR.

3. Accordingly, in supersession of clarifications and FAQs issued vide General Circular no. 21/2014 (dated 18th June 2014), 36/2014 (dated 17th September 2014), 01/2016 (dated 12th January 2016), 05/2016 (dated 16th May 2016), clarification issued vide letter dated 25.01.2018 and General Circular no. 06/2018 (dated 28th May 2018), a set of FAQs along with response of the Ministry is provided herewith at **Annexure** for better understanding and facilitating effective implementation of CSR.

4. This issues with the approval of competent authority.

Yours faithfully,

(Shobhit Srivastava)
Deputy Director (CSR Cell)

Copy to:

1. **E-Governance for uploading on MCA website**
2. **Guard File.**

Annexure

Frequently Asked Questions (FAQs) on Corporate Social Responsibility (CSR)

S. No.	*Question*	*Answer*
1.0	**Applicability of CSR**	
1.1	Which companies qualify for CSR under the Companies Act, 2013?	A company satisfying any of the following criteria during the immediately preceding financial year is required to comply with CSR provisions specified under section 135(1) of the Companies Act, 2013 read with the Companies (CSR Policy) Rules, 2014 made thereunder: (i) net worth of rupees five hundred crore or more, or (ii) turnover of rupees one thousand crore or more, or (iii) net profit of rupees five crore or more.
1.2	Whether a holding or subsidiary of a company fulfilling the criteria under section 135(1) has to comply with the provisions of section 135, even if the holding or subsidiary itself does not fulfil the criteria?	No, the compliance with CSR requirements is specific to each company. A holding or subsidiary of a company is not required to comply with the CSR provisions unless the holding or subsidiary itself fulfils the eligibility criteria prescribed under section 135(1) stated above. **Example:** Company A is covered under the criteria mentioned in section 135(1). Company B is holding company of company A. If Company B by itself does not satisfy any of the criteria mentioned in section 135(1), Company B is not required to comply with the provisions of section 135.
1.3	Whether provisions of CSR are applicable to a section 8 Company?	Yes, section 135(1) of the Act commences with the words "Every company...." and thus applies to section 8 companies as well.
1.4	Whether CSR provisions apply to a company that has not completed the period of three financial years since its incorporation?	Yes. If the company has not completed three financial years since its incorporation, but it satisfies any of the criteria mentioned in section 135(1), the CSR provisions including spending of at least two per cent of the average net profits made during immediately preceding financial year(s) are applicable. **Example:** Company A is incorporated during FY 2018-19, and as per eligibility criteria the company is covered under section 135(1) for FY 2020-21. The CSR spending obligation under section 135(5) for Company A would be at least two per

S. No.	Question	Answer	
		cent of the average net profits of the company made during FY 2018-19 and FY 2019-20.	
2.0	**CSR Framework**		
2.1	What is the composition of the CSR Committee?	The composition of the CSR Committee for various categories of companies is as under:	
		Listed companies	Three or more directors, out of which at least one shall be an independent director.
		Unlisted public companies	Three or more directors, out of which at least one shall be an independent director. However, if there is no requirement of having an independent director in the company, two or more directors.
		Private companies	Two or more directors. No independent directors are required as mentioned in the proviso under section 135(1).
		Foreign company	At least two persons out of which: (a) one shall be as specified under clause (d) of sub- section (1) of section 380 of the Act, and (b) another shall be nominated by the foreign company. *(Refer rule 5(1) of the Companies (CSR Policy) Rules, 2014)*
		Where the amount required to be spent by a company on CSR does not exceed fifty lakh rupees, the requirement for constitution of the CSR Committee is not mandatory and the functions of the CSR Committee, in such cases, shall be discharged by the Board of Directors of the company.	
2.2	What are the functions of the CSR Committee?	The Corporate Social Responsibility Committee shall — (i) formulate and recommend the CSR policy to the Board; (ii) recommend the amount of expenditure to be incurred on CSR activities; (iii) monitor the CSR policy of the company from time to time; and (iv) formulate and recommend to the Board, an annual action plan in pursuance of its CSR policy, which shall include the items as	

S. No.	*Question*	*Answer*
		mentioned in rule 5(2) of the Companies (CSR Policy) Rules, 2014. For companies covered under Section 135(9) of the Act and not required to have CSR Committee, these functions shall be carried out by the Board itself.
2.3	What are the responsibilities of the Board in relation to the CSR provisions?	CSR is a Board-driven process. The responsibilities of the Board of a CSR-eligible company, inter-alia, include the following: (i) approve the CSR policy; (ii) disclose contents of such policy in its report and also place it on the company's website, if any; (iii) ensure that the activities included in the CSR policy are undertaken by the company; (iv) ensure that the company spends, in every financial year, at least two per cent of the average net profits of the company made during the three immediately preceding financial years; (v) satisfy itself regarding the utilisation of the disbursed CSR funds; and (vi) if the company fails to spend at least two per cent of the average net profits of the company, the Board shall, in its report made under clause (o) of sub-section (3) of section 134, specify the reasons for not spending the amount and transfer the unspent CSR amount as per provisions of sections 135(5) and 135(6) of the Act.
2.4	What is the role of the Government in the approval and implementation of the CSR pro-grammes/projects of a company?	Provisions of section 135, read with Schedule VII of the Act and Companies (CSR Policy) Rules, 2014 provide the broad framework within which the eligible companies are required to formulate their CSR policies including activities to be undertaken and implementation of the same. CSR is a board-driven process, and the Board of the company is empowered to plan, approve, execute, and monitor the CSR activities of the company based on the recommendation of its CSR Committee. The Government has no direct role in the approval and implementation of the CSR programmes/ projects of a company.

S. No.	*Question*	*Answer*
2.5	What are the mechanisms for monitoring the CSR process?	CSR is a Board-driven process, and the Board of the company is empowered to plan, decide, execute, and monitor the CSR activities of the company based on the recommendation of its CSR Committee. The CSR architecture is disclosure-based and CSR-mandated companies are required to file details of CSR activities annually in MCA21 registry. Companies are required to make necessary disclosures in the financial statements regarding CSR including non-compliance. The existing legal provisions such as mandatory disclosures, accountability of the CSR Committee and the Board, and provisions for audit of accounts of the company provide sufficient mechanisms for monitoring.
2.6	What is the role of the Government in monitoring compliance of CSR provisions by companies?	The Government monitors the compliance of CSR provisions through the disclosures made by the companies in the MCA 21 portal. For any violation of CSR provisions, action can be initiated by the Government against such non-compliant companies as per provisions of the Companies Act, 2013 after due examination of records, and following due process of law. Non- compliance of CSR provisions has been notified as a civil wrong w.e.f. 22nd January, 2021.
3.0	**CSR Expenditure**	
3.1	How is average net profit calculated for the purpose of section 135 of the Act? Whether 'profit before tax' or 'profit after tax' is used for such computation?	The average net profit for the purpose of determining the spending on CSR activities is to be computed in accordance with the provisions of section 198 of the Act and will also be exclusive of the items given under rule 2(1)(h) of the Companies (CSR Policy) Rules, 2014. Section 198 of the Act specifies certain additions/deletions (adjustments) to be made while calculating the net profit of a company (mainly it excludes capital payments/receipts, income tax, set-off of past losses). Profit Before Tax (PBT) is used for computation of net profit under section 135 of the Act.
3.2	What is the meaning of the term 'administrative overheads'? What is the maximum permissible limit for administrative overheads?	Administrative overheads are the expenses incurred by the company for 'general management and administration' of CSR functions. However, the expenses which are directly incurred for the designing, implementation, monitoring, and evaluation of a particular CSR project or

S. No.	*Question*	*Answer*
		programme, shall not be included in the administrative overheads. Administrative overheads generally comprise of items such as employee costs, utilities, office supplies, legal expenses, etc. However, expenses which are attributed to the project implementation shall be included in project cost only. **Example:** Salary and training for the employees working in the CSR division of a company, stationery cost, travelling expenses, etc. may be categorised as administrative overheads. However, salary of school teachers or other staff, etc. for education-related CSR projects shall be covered under education project cost. The maximum permissible limit for administrative overheads is five per cent of the total CSR expenditure of the company for the financial year.
3.3	Are administrative overheads applicable only for expenses incurred by the company, or can they be applied to expenses incurred by the implementing agency as well?	According to rule 2(1)(b) of the Companies (CSR Policy) Rules, 2014, administrative overheads mean the expenses incurred by the company in the general management and administration of CSR functions in the company. Therefore, expenses incurred by implementing agencies on the management of CSR activities shall not amount to administrative overheads and cannot be claimed by the company.
3.4	What is the meaning of surplus arising from CSR activities? How can this surplus be utilised?	Surplus refers to income generated from the spend on CSR activities, e.g., interest income earned by the implementing agency on funds provided under CSR, revenue received from the CSR projects, disposal/sale of materials used in CSR projects, and other similar income sources. The surplus arising out of CSR activities shall be utilised only for CSR purposes.
3.5	Whether contribution to the corpus of an entity is an admissible CSR expenditure?	No, the provision relating to contribution to corpus as admissible CSR expenditure has been amended and the contribution to corpus of any entity is not an admissible CSR expenditure w.e.f. 22nd January, 2021.
3.6	Whether expenses related to transfer of capital asset as provided under rule 7(4) of Companies (CSR Policy) Rules, 2014, will qualify as admissible CSR expenditure?	Yes, the expenses relating to transfer of capital asset such as stamp duty and registration fees, will qualify as admissible CSR expenditure in the year of such transfer.

S. No.	Question	Answer
3.7	If a company spends more than the requirement provided under section 135, can that excess amount be set off against the mandatory 2% CSR expenditure in succeeding financial years?	Yes, the excess amount can be set off against the required 2% CSR expenditure up to the immediately succeeding three financial years subject to compliance with the conditions stipulated under rule 7(3) of the Companies (CSR Policy) Rules, 2014. This position is applicable from 22nd January, 2021 and has a prospective effect. Thus, no carry forward shall be allowed for the excess amount spent, if any, in financial years prior to FY 2020-21.
3.8	If a company cannot take the benefit of set off of excess amount spent in the previous financial year because of non-applicability of CSR provisions, will the excess amount lapse?	Yes, the law states that the excess CSR amount spent can be carried forward up to immediately succeeding three financial years; thus, in case any excess amount is left for set off, it will lapse at the end of the said period. **Example:** In FY 2020-21 a company had spent Rs. 2 crores in excess. In FY 2021-22, it sets-off Rs. 50 lakhs from such excess. However, from FY 2022-23, the company is no longer subject to CSR provisions under section 135(1). In such case, the company may continue to retain the remaining excess CSR of Rs. 1.50 crores up to FY 2023-24, and thereafter the same shall lapse.
3.9	Whether it is mandatory for companies to carry out CSR in their local areas?	The first proviso to section 135(5) of the Act provides that the company shall give preference to local areas and the areas around where it operates. Some activities in Schedule VII such as welfare activities for war widows, art and culture, and other similar activities, transcend geographical boundaries and are applicable across the country. With the advent of Information & Communication Technology (ICT) and emergence of new age businesses like e-commerce companies, process-outsourcing companies, and aggregator companies, it is becoming increasingly difficult to determine the local area of various activities. The spirit of the Act is to ensure that CSR initiatives are aligned with the national priorities and enhance engagement of the corporate sector towards achieving Sustainable Development Goals (SDGs). Thus, the preference to local area in the Act is only directory and not mandatory in nature and companies need to balance local area preference with national priorities.

S. No.	*Question*	*Answer*
3.10	Whether CSR expenditure of a company can be claimed as a business expenditure?	No, the amount spent by a company towards CSR cannot be claimed as business expenditure. Explanation 2 to section 37(1) of the Income Tax Act, 1961 which was inserted through the Finance Act, 2014 provides that any expenditure incurred by an assessee on the activities relating to CSR referred to in section 135 of the Companies Act, 2013 shall not be deemed to be an expenditure incurred by the assessee for the purposes of the business or profession.
3.11	What tax benefits can be availed under CSR?	No specific tax exemptions have been extended to CSR expenditure. The Finance Act, 2014 also clarifies that expenditure on CSR does not form part of business expenditure.
3.12	Whether contribution in kind can be monetized to be shown as CSR expenditure?	The requirement comes from section 135(5) that states that "The Board of every company shall ensure that it spends...." Therefore, CSR contribution cannot be in kind and monetized.
3.13	Can CSR expenditure be incurred on activities beyond Schedule VII?	No, CSR expenditure cannot be incurred on activities beyond Schedule VII of the Act. The activities undertaken in pursuance of the CSR policy must be relatable to Schedule VII of the Companies Act, 2013. The items enlisted in Schedule VII of the Act are broad-based and are intended to cover a wide range of activities. The entries in the said Schedule VII must be interpreted liberally to capture the essence of the subjects enumerated in the said Schedule.
3.14	What are the different modes of incurring CSR expenditure?	CSR expenditure can be incurred in multiple modes: (i) 'Activities route', which is a direct mode wherein a company undertakes the CSR projects or programmes as per Schedule VII of the Act, either by itself or by engaging implementing agencies as prescribed in Companies (CSR Policy) Rules, 2014. (ii) 'Contribution to funds route', which allows the contributions to various funds as specified in Schedule VII of the Act. (iii) Contribution to incubators and R&D projects, as specified in item (ix)(a) and contribution to institutes/organisations, engaged in research and development activity, as specified under item (ix)(b) of Schedule VII of the Act.

S. No.	Question	Answer
3.15	Which are the funds specified in Schedule VII of the Act for the purpose of CSR contribution?	Contributions to the following funds shall be admissible as CSR expenditure: (i) Swachh Bharat Kosh (ii) Clean Ganga Fund (iii) Prime Minister's National Relief Fund (PMNRF) (iv) Prime Minister's Citizen Assistance and Relief in Emergency Situations Fund (PM CARES Fund) (v) Any other fund set up by the Central Government and notified by the Ministry of Corporate Affairs, for socio-economic development and relief and welfare of the Scheduled Castes, the Scheduled Tribes, other backward classes, minorities and women.
3.16	Will contribution to any other fund set up for carrying out the activities mentioned in Schedule VII of the Act, be an admissible CSR expenditure?	No, the Act does not recognise any contribution to any other fund, which is not specifically mentioned in Schedule VII, as an admissible CSR expenditure.
3.17	Can CSR funds be utilised to fund Government schemes?	The objective of CSR provisions is to involve the corporates as partners in the social development process. Use of corporate innovations and management skills in the delivery of 'public goods' is at the core of CSR implementation by the companies. Therefore, CSR should not be interpreted as a source of financing the resource gaps in Government Schemes. However, the Board of the eligible company may undertake similar activities independently subject to fulfilment of Companies (CSR Policy) Rules, 2014.
3.18	Whether involvement of employees of a company in their CSR projects can be monetized and accounted for under the head of 'CSR expenditure'?	No, involvement of employees in CSR projects of a company cannot be monetized. Contribution and involvement of employees in CSR activities of the company will no doubt generate interest/ pride in CSR work and promote transformation from Corporate Social Responsibility (CSR) as an obligation to Socially Responsible Corporate (SRC) in all aspects of their functioning. Companies, therefore, should be encouraged to involve their employees in CSR activities.

S. No.	*Question*	*Answer*
4.0	**CSR Activities**	
4.1	Which activities do not qualify as eligible CSR activity?	Rule 2(1)(d) of the Companies (CSR Policy) Rules, 2014 defines CSR and the following activities are specifically excluded from being considered as eligible CSR activity: (i) Activities undertaken in pursuance of normal course of business of the company. However, exemption is provided for three financial years, till FY 2022-23, to companies engaged in R&D activities for new vaccines, drugs, and medical devices in their normal course of business, related to COVID-19. This exclusion is allowed only in case the companies are engaged in R&D in collaboration with organisations as mentioned in item (ix) of Schedule VII and disclose the same in their Board reports. (ii) Activities undertaken outside India, except for training of Indian sports personnel representing any State or Union Territory at national level or India at international level; (iii) Contribution of any amount, directly or indirectly, to any political party under section 182 of the Act; (iv) Activities benefitting employees of the company as defined in section 2(k) of the Code on Wages, 2019; (v) Sponsorship activities for deriving marketing benefits for products/services; (vi) Activities for fulfilling statutory obligations under any law in force in India.
4.2	Whether the companies can undertake any CSR activity mentioned under Schedule VII of the Act for the exclusive benefit of their employees, workers and their family members?	Rule 2(1)(d)(iv) of the Companies (CSR Policy) Rules, 2014 states that any activity benefitting employees of the company shall not be considered as eligible CSR activity. As per the rule, any activity designed exclusively for the benefit of employees shall be considered as an "activity benefitting employees" and will not qualify as permissible CSR expenditure. The spirit behind any CSR activity is to benefit the public at large and the activity should be non- discriminatory to any class of beneficiaries. However, any activity which is not designed to benefit employees solely, but the public at large, and if the employees and their family members are incidental beneficiaries, then, such activity would not be considered as

S. No.	*Question*	*Answer*
		"activity benefitting employees" and will qualify as eligible CSR activity.
4.3	What is the meaning of sponsorship activities deriving marketing benefits for company's products or services?	Sponsorship activities of an event are done with an aim of deriving marketing benefits for a company's product or services. The intent of CSR is to encourage companies to undertake the activities in a project or programme mode rather than as a one-off event. Companies shall not use CSR purely as a marketing or brand building tool for their business, but brand building as a collateral benefit does not vitiate the spirit of CSR.
4.4	Are activities undertaken by companies outside India for the benefit of resident Indians, permitted as eligible CSR activity?	Rule 2(1)(d)(ii) of the Companies (CSR Policy) Rules, 2014 clearly states that any activity undertaken by the company outside India shall not be an eligible CSR activity. The only exception is training of Indian sports personnel representing any State or Union Territory at national or international level.
4.5	How can companies with small CSR funds take up CSR activities in a project mode?	A well-designed CSR project can be managed with small CSR funds as well. Further, there is a provision in the Companies (CSR Policy) Rules, 2014 that enables such companies to collaborate with other companies for undertaking CSR activities by way of pooling their CSR resources. (*Refer rule 4(4) in Companies (CSR Policy) Rules, 2014*).
5.0	**CSR Implementation**	
5.1	What are the different modes of implementation of CSR activities?	Pursuant to rule 4 of the Companies (CSR Policy) Rules, 2014 a company may undertake CSR activities through following three modes of implementation: (i) Implementation by the company itself (ii) Implementation through eligible implementing agencies as prescribed under sub-rule (1) of rule 4. (iii) Implementation in collaboration with one or more companies as prescribed under sub-rule (4) of rule 4.
5.2	Which entities are eligible to act as an implementing agency for undertaking CSR activities?	Rule 4(1) of the Companies (CSR Policy) Rules, 2014 provides the eligible entities which can act as an implementing agency for undertaking CSR activities. These are: (i) Entity established by the company itself or along with any other company – a company established under section 8 of the Act, or a

S. No.	*Question*	*Answer*
		registered public trust or a registered society, registered under section 12A and 80G of the Income Tax Act, 1961. (ii) Entity established by the Central Government or State Government – a company established under section 8 of the Act, or a registered trust or a registered society. (iii) Statutory bodies – any entity established under an Act of Parliament or a State legislature. (iv) Other bodies – a company established under section 8 of the Act, or a registered public trust or a registered society, registered under section 12A and 80G of the Income Tax Act, 1961, and having an established track record of at least three years in undertaking similar activities.
5.3	Whether all three types of entities – a company established under section 8 of the Act, or a registered public trust, or a registered society, are required to have income-tax registration u/s 12A as well as 80G of the Income Tax Act, 1961?	Yes, as per rule 4(1) all three types of entities – a company established under section 8 of the Act, or a registered public trust, or a registered society are required to have income-tax registration u/s 12A as well as 80G of the Income Tax Act, 1961 to act as implementing agency, except for any entities established by Central or State Government.
5.4	What is meant by 'registered public trusts' in such states where registration is not mandatory?	Registered public trust (as referred to in rule 4(1) of the Companies (CSR Policy) Rules, 2014) would include trusts registered under the Income Tax Act, 1961 in respect of those states where registration of public trusts is not mandatory.
5.5	What is the purpose of registration of the implementing agency on MCA21 portal?	The identification of suitable implementing agencies is a major concern for companies. Registration of implementing agencies on MCA21 portal is aimed at creating a database of such agencies for companies who may want to engage them. Further, this will bring accountability and transparency in the implementation of CSR activities and thereby strengthen the CSR eco-system.
5.6	Is it mandatory for every implementing agency to register on the MCA21 portal?	Yes, every implementing agency mentioned in rule 4(1) of the Companies (CSR Policy) Rules, 2014 shall mandatorily register itself in the MCA21 portal w.e.f. 01st April 2021 in order to enable it to undertake CSR activities on behalf of the company.

S. No.	*Question*	*Answer*
5.7	Whether an ongoing project approved prior to April 01, 2021, may be implemented by an implementing agency not registered on MCA21 portal?	Since the requirement of registration has commenced from 01st April, 2021, any ongoing project which has been approved between 22nd January, 2021 and 31st March, 2021, may be carried out by an implementing agency which is not registered in MCA21 portal. However, the unregistered implementing agency is required to register in MCA21 portal before undertaking any new project after 01st April, 2021.
5.8	Whether registration of implementing agency by filing e-form CSR-1 is mandatory in case the company carries out CSR activities directly?	No. The question of filing e-form CSR-1 does not arise in case the company carries out CSR activities directly.
5.9	Can international organisations act as an implementing agency?	No, an international organisation cannot act as an implementing agency.
5.10	What is the role of international organisations in the context of CSR?	Pursuant to rule 4(3) of the Companies (CSR Policy) Rules, 2014, a company can engage international organisations for the limited purposes of designing, monitoring, and evaluation of the CSR projects or programmes, or for capacity building of personnel of the company involved in CSR activities.
6.0	**Ongoing Project**	
6.1	What is the meaning of 'ongoing project'? Which projects can be considered as ongoing?	Ongoing project has been defined under rule 2(1)(i) of the Companies (CSR Policy) Rules, 2014 as: (i) a multi-year project, stretching over more than one financial year; (ii) having a timeline not exceeding three years excluding the year of commencement; (iii) includes such project that was initially not approved as a multi-year project but whose duration has been extended beyond one year by the Board based on reasonable justification. The project should have commenced within the financial year to be termed as 'ongoing'. The intent is to include a project which has an identifiable commencement and completion dates. After the completion of any ongoing project, the Board of the company is free to design any other project related to operation and maintenance of such completed projects in a manner as may be deemed fit on a case-to-case basis. ***Note:*** *The term 'year' refers to financial year as defined in section 2(41) of the Act.*

S. No.	*Question*	*Answer*
6.2	When will an ongoing project be regarded as 'commenced'?	An ongoing project will have 'commenced' when the company has either issued the work order pertaining to the project or awarded the contract for execution of the project.
6.3	What is the maximum permissible time period for any ongoing project? Can the time period of an ongoing project be extended beyond the permissible period?	As per the definition of an ongoing project, the maximum permissible time period shall be three financial years excluding the financial year in which it is commenced i.e. (1+3) financial years. Under no circumstances shall the time period of an ongoing project be extended beyond its permissible limit.
6.4	What are the responsibilities of the Board in case ongoing projects are undertaken by the company?	In case of ongoing projects, the major responsibilities of the Board, inter-alia, include: (i) identification of the ongoing projects; (ii) year-wise allocation of funds; (iii) transferring the unspent money to a separate bank account as prescribed under sub-section (6) of section 135; (iv) monitoring the implementation of the projects with reference to the approved timelines and year-wise allocation; and (v) making modifications, if any, for smooth implementation of the projects within the overall permissible time period.
6.5	Can ongoing projects be implemented through implementing agencies?	Yes, once the Board approves a project as an ongoing project, then it can choose to implement the project either itself, or through any of the implementing agencies as mentioned in rule 4(1) of the Companies (CSR Policy) Rules, 2014.
6.6	Does the Board have the power to abandon or modify an ongoing project within the permissible period of three years?	As per provisions of the CSR Rules, the Board may abandon or modify an ongoing project, partially or wholly, under exceptional circumstances, during the prescribed project period as per the recommendation of its CSR Committee, and by providing reasonable justification to that effect. It is important to keep in mind that the maximum permissible period for an ongoing project is three years excluding the year of its commencement.
6.7	Can funds earmarked for one project be used for another project?	Yes, the budget outlay dedicated for one project can be used against another project. In such a case, the Board and CSR Committee should appropriately record the alteration in the target spending and modify the same in accordance with the actuals.

<table>
<tr><th>S. No.</th><th>Question</th><th>Answer</th></tr>
<tr><td>7.0</td><td>Treatment of Unspent CSR Amount</td><td></td></tr>
<tr><td>7.1</td><td>What actions need to be taken if a company spends less than the amount required to be spent under CSR obligation in a particular year?</td><td>If a company spends less than the amount required to be spent under their CSR obligation, the Board shall specify the reasons for not spending in the Board's report and shall deal with the unspent amount in the following manner:
<table>
<tr><th>Nature of unspent amount</th><th>Action required</th><th>Timelines</th></tr>
<tr><td>Unspent amount pertains to 'ongoing projects'</td><td>Transfer such unspent amount to a separate bank account of the company to be called as 'Unspent CSR Account'.</td><td>Within 30 days from the end of the financial year.</td></tr>
<tr><td>Unspent amount pertains to 'other than ongoing projects'</td><td>Transfer unspent amount to any fund included in Schedule VII of the Act.</td><td>Within 6 months from the end of the financial year.</td></tr>
</table></td></tr>
<tr><td>7.2</td><td>Where the company was unable to meet its CSR obligation, but transferred the said unspent amount to any fund included in Schedule VII of the Act, will the same be considered as compliance under section 135?</td><td>The compliance of CSR is fulfilled when the company spends the prescribed amount as per its obligation. However, in case the company fails to spend the requisite amount within the financial year, it shall fulfil its obligation by transferring the unspent amount to any fund included in Schedule VII of the Act. The same will be considered as compliance with section 135(5) of the Act. Further, the Board of the company is required to give the requisite disclosure in the Board report and annual report on CSR.</td></tr>
<tr><td>7.3</td><td>A company has been given six months' time to transfer the unspent CSR amount, other than the amount pertaining to ongoing projects, to any fund included in Schedule VII of the Act. Can the company spend this amount in the said period of six months on any CSR activity?</td><td>No, companies are not permitted to spend the unspent CSR amount, other than the amount pertaining to ongoing projects, on any CSR activity during the intervening period of six months after the end of the financial year. Such unspent CSR amount is required to be transferred to any fund included in Schedule VII of the Act.</td></tr>
<tr><td>7.4</td><td>Whether disbursal of funds by a company to the implementing agency for the implementation of projects will be considered as spend under section 135(5) and rules made there under?</td><td>Section 135(5) of the Act prescribes minimum spending obligation for the company. The company may fulfil its CSR spending obligation directly by itself or though engaging an implementing agency. The implementing agency acts on behalf of the company and mere disbursal of funds</td></tr>
</table>

S. No.	*Question*	*Answer*
		for implementation of a project does not amount to spending unless the implementing agency utilises the whole amount. In the annual action plan, the CSR Committee of the company is required to provide for modalities of utilisation of funds. The CSR Committee shall recommend to the Board on budget allocation for any CSR project including modalities of utilisation of funds in every project. Further, as per rule 4(5) of the Companies (CSR Policy) Rules, 2014, the Board of a company shall satisfy itself that the funds so disbursed have been utilised for the purposes and in the manner as approved by it and the Chief Financial Officer or the person responsible for financial management shall certify to the effect. Accordingly, the CSR Committee and Board should ensure that CSR fund should be disbursed to implementing agencies, partially or wholly, in such a manner so that they can be utilised by them during the financial year. Mere disbursal of funds for implementation of a project does not amount to spending unless the implementing agency utilises the whole amount.
7.5	Should a company open a separate 'Unspent CSR Account' for each ongoing project?	No, a company can open a single special account, called 'Unspent Corporate Social Responsibility Account', for a financial year in any scheduled bank, to transfer the unspent amount w.r.t ongoing project(s) of that financial year. A company needs to open a separate 'Unspent CSR Account' for each financial year but not for each ongoing project.
7.6	Can the amount transferred to 'Unspent CSR Account' of the company be utilised for regular business of the company?	No, the provisioning of a separate special account, namely the 'Unspent CSR Account', in any scheduled bank is to ensure that the unspent amount, if any, is transferred to this designated account and used only for meeting the expenses of ongoing projects, and not for other general purposes of the company. The special account cannot be used by the company as collaterals or creating a charge or any other business activity.
7.7	Can an ongoing project initiated by a company in any previous financial year (for instance in FY 2019-20) be classified as an ongoing project under section 135(6) of the Act. Is the	No, the provisions related to ongoing projects have come into effect from 22nd January 2021, i.e., from FY 2020-21 onwards. The said provisions are prospective in effect and not applicable to projects of previous financial years.

S. No.	*Question*	*Answer*
	unspent amount of previous financial years also required to be transferred to the Unspent CSR Account?	Further, the Board of the company is free to decide the treatment of the unspent CSR amount of previous financial years prior to FY 2020-21. The Board can either transfer the amount to 'Unspent CSR Account' or continue as per the previous accounting practices adopted by the company.
8.0	**CSR Enforcement**	
8.1	What are the penal provisions for non-compliance with the provisions regarding transfer of unspent amount?	The said non-compliance is a civil wrong and shall attract the following penalties: **Company**: Twice the unspent amount required to be transferred to any fund included in Schedule VII of the Act or Unspent CSR Account, as the case may be, or one crore rupees, whichever is less. **Every Officer in Default**: 1/10th of the unspent amount required to be transferred to any fund included in Schedule VII of the Act or Unspent CSR Account, or two lakh rupees, whichever is less.
8.2	Will the penal proceedings apply even after the unspent amount has been transferred to the Unspent CSR Account or to the funds mentioned in Schedule VII of the Act?	The penalty does not relieve the company from the obligations under the law, and the penalty is over and above the obligated amount required to be transferred under section 135(5) or 135(6). The penalty is the consequence of not abiding by the law, and not an alternative for the same.
8.3	Is the penal provision in section 135(7) specific to non-transference of the unspent CSR amount?	Yes, section 135(7) clearly states the penalty for default in complying with the provisions of sub-section (5) or sub- section (6) only.
8.4	What are the penal provisions relating to non-compliance with provisions other than sections 135(5) and 135(6) of the Act?	In case of non-compliance with any other provisions of the section or rules, the provisions of section 134(8) or general penalty under section 450 of the Act will be applicable. Further, in case of non-payment of penalty within the stipulated period, the provisions of section 454(8) will be applicable.
9.0	**Impact Assessment**	
9.1	What is the objective of providing impact assessment of CSR activities?	The purpose of impact assessment is to assess the social impact of a particular CSR project. The intent is to encourage companies to take considered decisions before deploying CSR amounts and assess the impact of their CSR spending. This not only serves as feedback for companies to plan and allocate resources better but shall also deepen the impact of CSR.

S. No.	*Question*	*Answer*
9.2	Which companies are required to undertake impact assessment?	Rule 8(3) of the Companies (CSR Policy) Rules, 2014 mandates following class of companies to conduct impact assessment: (i) companies with minimum average CSR obligation of Rs. 10 crore or more in the immediately preceding 3 financial years; and (ii) companies that have CSR projects with outlays of minimum Rs. 1 crore and which have been completed not less than 1 year before undertaking impact assessment. Impact assessment shall be carried out project-wise only in cases where both the above conditions are fulfilled. In other cases, it can be taken up by the company on a voluntary basis.
9.3	Whether companies are required to undertake impact assessment for FY 2020-21?	The provisions for impact assessment have come into effect from 22nd January, 2021. Accordingly, the company is required to undertake impact assessment of the CSR projects completed on or after January 22, 2021. However, as a good practice the Board may undertake impact assessment of completed projects of previous financial years.
9.4	Who can conduct impact assessment?	Rule 8(3) of the Companies (CSR Policy) Rules, 2014 requires that the impact assessment be conducted by an independent agency. The Board has the prerogative to decide on the eligibility criteria for selection of the independent agency for impact assessment.
9.5	Is expenditure on impact assessment over and above the administrative overheads of 5%, or included in the same?	Yes, the expenditure incurred on impact assessment is over and above the specified administrative overheads of 5%. Expenditure up to a maximum of 5% of the total CSR expenditure for that financial year or 50 lakh rupees (whichever is lower) can be incurred separately for impact assessment.
9.6	Whether impact assessment reports of all the CSR projects shall be annexed to the annual report on CSR?	Rule 8(3)(b) of the Companies (CSR Policy) Rules, 2014 provides that impact assessment reports shall be placed before the Board and shall be annexed to the report on CSR. It is clarified that web-link to access the complete impact assessment reports and providing executive summary of the impact assessment reports in the annual report on CSR, shall be considered as sufficient compliance of the said rule.

S. No.	*Question*	*Answer*
9.7	When two or more companies collaborate for implementation of a CSR project, should the impact assessment carried out by one company be shared with other companies?	Yes, in case two or more companies choose to collaborate for the implementation of a CSR project, then the impact assessment carried out by one company for the common project may be shared with the other companies for the purpose of disclosure to the Board and in the annual report on CSR. The sharing of the cost of impact assessment may be decided by the collaborating companies subject to the limit as prescribed in rule 8(3)(c) of the Companies (CSR Policy) Rules, 2014 for each company.
10.0	**CSR Reporting & Disclosure**	
10.1	Whether reporting of CSR is mandatory in Board's Report?	Yes, as per rule 8(1) of the Companies (CSR Policy) Rules, 2014, the Board's Report pertaining to any financial year, for a CSR-eligible company, shall include an annual report on CSR containing particulars specified in Annexure I or Annexure II of the said rules, as applicable.
10.2	Is it mandatory for foreign companies to give reports on CSR activities?	Yes, as per rule 8(2) of the Companies (CSR Policy) Rules, 2014, in case of a CSR-eligible foreign company, the balance sheet filed under clause (b) of sub-section (1) of section 381 of the Act, shall include an annual report on CSR containing particulars specified in Annexure I or Annexure II of the said rules, as applicable.
10.3	What are the disclosure requirements on the website of the company?	As per rule 9, the Board of Directors of the company shall mandatorily disclose the following on their website, if any, for public access: (i) Composition of the CSR Committee; (ii) CSR Policy; and (iii) Projects approved by the Board.
10.4	Whether every CSR project irrespective of outlay and percentage to the total CSR expenditure of the company needs to be disclosed on the website of the respective company in terms of rule 9 of the Companies (CSR Policy) Rules, 2014?	Yes, as per rule 9 of the Companies (CSR Policy) Rules, 2014, all CSR projects approved by the Board are required to be disclosed on the website of the company, if any, for public access.

APPENDIX 3

भारत का राजपत्र
The Gazette of India

सी.जी.-डी.एल.-अ.-21092022-238956
CG-DL-E-21092022-238956

असाधारण
EXTRAORDINARY

भाग II—खण्ड 3—उप-खण्ड (i)
PART II—Section 3—Sub-section (i)

प्राधिकार से प्रकाशित
PUBLISHED BY AUTHORITY

सं. 634] नई दिल्ली, मंगलवार, सितम्बर 20, 2022/भाद्र 29, 1944
No. 634] NEW DELHI, TUESDAY, SEPTEMBER 20, 2022/BHADRA 29, 1944

कारपोरेट कार्य मंत्रालय

अधिसूचना

नई दिल्ली, 20 सितम्बर, 2022

सा.का.नि. 715(अ).—केंद्रीय सरकार, कंपनी अधिनियम, 2013 (2013 का 18) की धारा 135 और धारा 469 की उप-धारा (1) और उप-धारा (2) के द्वारा प्रदत्त शक्तियों का प्रयोग करते हुए, कंपनी (कारपोरेट सामाजिक दायित्व नीति) नियम, 2014 का और संशोधन करने के लिए निम्नलिखित नियम बनाती है, अर्थात्:-

1. संक्षिप्त नाम और प्रारंभ - (1) इन नियमों का संक्षिप्त नाम कंपनी (कारपोरेट सामाजिक दायित्व नीति) संशोधन नियम, 2022 है।

(2) ये राजपत्र में इनके प्रकाशन की तारीख को प्रवृत्त होंगे।

2. कंपनी (कारपोरेट सामाजिक दायित्व नीति) नियम, 2014 (जिसे इसमें इसके पश्चात उक्त नियम कहा गया है) में, नियम 3 में,-

(i) उपनियम (1) में, परन्तुक के पश्चात, निम्नलिखित परन्तुक अंतःस्थापित किया जाएगा, अर्थात:-

"परंतु यह और कि कोई कंपनी, जिसकी धारा 135 की उपधारा (6) के अनुसार, अपने अव्ययित कारपोरेट सामाजिक दायित्व खाते में, किसी प्रकार की राशि है तो वह सीएसआर समिति का गठन करेगी और उक्त धारा की उपधारा (2) से (6) में विहित उपबंधों का अनुपालन करेगी";

6273 GI/2022 (1)

MINISTRY OF CORPORATE AFFAIRS

NOTIFICATION

New Delhi, the 20th September 2022

G.S.R. 715(E)

Amendment to Rule 3

Rule 3 of Companies (CSR Policy) Rules has been amended such that every company including its holding or subsidiary and a foreign company defined under Section 2(42) of the Indian Companies Act, having its branch office or project office in India and which fulfils the criteria specified under section 135(1) of the Indian Companies Act 2013 (i.e., Net Worth of Rs. 500/- crore or more or Turnover of Rs. 1,000/- crore or more or Net Profit of Rs. 5 crore or more, during the immediately preceding financial year) **shall constitute a CSR committee and comply with the provisions of spending CSR funds, if the company has any amount in its 'Unspent Corporate Social Responsibility Account'.**

Sub-rule (2) of Rule 3 has been omitted and the inference is even if a company ceases to be covered u/s 135(1) (i.e., does not have for three consecutive financial years, Net Worth of Rs. 500/ - crore or more or Turnover of Rs. 1,000/- crore or more or Net Profit of Rs. 5 crore or more, during the immediately preceding financial year) **it will still be required to constitute a CSR Committee of the Board and comply with the requirements of Section 135.**

Amendment to Rule 4

Rule 4 has been amended to also recognize trusts, societies and section 8 companies registered under Section 10(23C) (iv), (v), (vi) or (vii) (educational and medical institutions) of Income Tax as eligible CSR implementing agencies. Till this very recent amendment, only trusts, societies and section 8 companies registered u/s 12A (now 12AB) of Income Tax were recognized.

Explanation to Rule 4 clarifies that "**any entity**" (established under an Act of Parliament or a State legislature) shall mean "a statutory body constituted under an Act of Parliament or State legislature to undertake (CSR) activities covered in Schedule VII of the Act."

Amendment to Rule 8

Rule 8 requires every company having average CSR obligation of ten crore rupees or more in pursuance of section 135(5) of the Act, in the three immediately preceding financial years, shall undertake impact assessment, through an independent agency, of their CSR projects having outlays of one crore rupees or more, and which have been completed not less than one year before undertaking the impact study.

Rule 8 has been amended such that a Company undertaking impact assessment may book the expenditure towards Corporate Social Responsibility for that financial year, which shall not exceed **two per cent** (earlier it was five per cent) of the total CSR expenditure for that financial year or fifty lakh rupees, **whichever is higher** (earlier it was whichever is less).

In other words, while the cap of five per cent has been reduced to two per cent, the cap of fifty lakh stands effectively relaxed especially for companies with high CSR expenditure outlays.

Annual Report on CSR

Format for the Annual Report on CSR Activities to be included in the Board's Report has also been amended to accommodate these changes.